HOWDY WAYFARER

NEW WAYS TO SUBSCRIBE

NOW ON SUBSTACK
WWW.WAYFARERMAGAZINE.COM

Howdy Good Wayfarers,

Sit down around the fire with us, we have some news to share! *The Wayfarer* is expanding into a weekly digital publication. We've launched *The Wayfarer* on Substack!

Since 2012, The Wayfarer has been offering literature, interviews, and art with the intention to inspire our readers, enrich their lives, and highlight the power for agency and change-making that each individual holds. By our definition, a wayfarer is one whose inner-compass is ever-oriented to truth, wisdom, healing, and beauty in their own wandering. Our mission as a publication is to foster a community of contemplative voices and provide readers with resources and perspectives that support them in their own journey.

In our effort to continually expand and evolve, we now offer several ways to subscribe!

- Free subscriptions (Access to Monthly public posts.)

- Paid on Subscription $5.00/mn or $50.00/yr

- Print Edition 1yr Subscription + a 1/yr Digital Subscription. 70.00/yr

- The paid Substack subscription will give unrestricted access to new features, poems, book reviews, recommendations, live readings, interviews; along with full access to the archive; and access to our new community chats.

- We will continue to release our biannual print edition

- Individual Past Print Issues are Available in paperback and ebook on our website as well as Amazon, B&N, Bookshop.org, and more.

Come explore and Subscribe!

Safe Journeys

—Wayfarer Staff

STAY WILD

READ

WAYFARER ECO-LIT SINCE 2012

FOUNDER AND EDITOR-IN-CHIEF

CONNOR WOLFE

MANAGING EDITOR

HEIDI BARR

SENIOR EDITORS

THEODORE RICHARDS

JASON KIRKEY

EDITORS-AT-LARGE

GAIL COLLINS-RANADIVE

IRIS GRAVILLE

FRANK INZAN OWEN

DAVID K. LEFF

THOMAS LLYOD QUALLS

KRISTEN WILLIAMS

ROBERT BRODER

AMY NAWROCKI

ERIC D. LEHMAN

CONTACT US

THE WAYFARER MAGAZINE
PO BOX 1601, NORTHAMPTON MA 01060
WAYFARER@HOMEBOUNDPUBLICATIONS.COM

SUBSCRIBE AT

WWW.WAYFARERMAGAZINE.COM OR WWW.WAYFARERBOOKS.ORG

ISSUE ISBN 978-1-956368-75-8
AVAILABLE IN PAPERBACK AND EBOOK
WHEREVER BOOKS ARE SOLD.

BASED IN THE BERKSHIRE MOUNTAINS, MASS.

Since 2012, *The Wayfarer Magazine* has been offering literature, interviews, and art with the intention to inspire our readers and highlight the power for agency and change-making that each individual holds. By our definition, a "wayfarer" is one whose inner compass is ever-oriented to truth, wisdom, healing, and beauty in their own wandering. *The Wayfarer's* mission as a publication is to foster a community of contemplative voices and provide readers with resources and perspectives that support them in their own journey.

About the Publisher Wayfarer Books we believe poetry is the language of the earth. We believe words, shaped like rivers through wild places, can change the shape of the world. We publish poets and writers and renegades who stand outside of mainstream culture—poets, essayists, and storytellers whose work might withstand the scrutiny of crows and coyotes, those who are cryptic and floral, the crepuscular, and the queer-at-heart. We are more than just a publisher but a community of writers. Our mission is to produce books that can serve as a compass and map to all wayfarers through wild terrain.

WWW.WAYFARERMAGAZINE.COM

THE EVOLUTION OF THE ARTIST
AN [EXTENDED] LETTER FROM THE EDITOR

BY CONNOR WOLFE THEY/THEM | EDITOR-IN-CHIEF, *THE WAYFARER*

I grew up in the design departments of newspapers and small magazines. My mother was a graphic designer. It was the 80s; the hair was big, the eye shadow was blue, the shoulder pads were towering, and women entered corporate America.

It was women who made up the design department for the regional paper my mother worked at, but a rotation of apathetic white men were always "the boss." The days I could go to work with her were golden—I was never bored. I can still remember sitting at her drafting table—my feet swinging freely below the stool while sketching my favorite subjects— mostly cartoon characters like Wile E. Coyote, Roadrunner, Snoopy, and Woodstock. When she was at the table, I watched her layout the individual pages of the daily paper by hand—using font books, border tape, clip art, and Indian ink. She kept a carousel of chisel-nib, double-ended markers of all colors and shades on her desk.

I remember going back to the newsroom here and there throughout my elementary years. The humming energy of the women's voices as they buzzed across the busy news floor, quieted, and the staccato of keystrokes replaced them. The open floors of drafting tables disappeared as the cubicle gridwork was pieced together. The carousel of markers was replaced by a corded mouse, which was attached to the first mass-produced Macintosh (Apple) Desktop.

The artists in the department dwindled as the computers replaced them one by one until only the head of the department stood alone, and my mother—along with the other graphic artists—moved into new careers with these now "obsolete" skills.

Right around the time the pink slips were handed out, my mother's own life unraveled, and we entered a period where we moved around a lot— staying wherever we could with friends and family—as she undertook the terrifying task of leaving my abusive stepfather. During this unhoused time, I didn't have my friends from the neighborhood or even her, really, as she left me at the family farm in rural upstate New York and then went to find new work (and to reconcile the difference between who her husband was and who she needed him to be).

In retrospect, the third grade was by far the most disjointed in my education. That year, I went to seven different schools—one school I just attended for a single day. But, somehow, in the turnstile of changing schools and towns and homes, there were still constants—one was my ring-bound multimedia sketch pad that I carried with me the way Linus carries his blue blanket, and the other was books—always books.

At every new school, there was an order of navigation. First, find the art room, then the cafeteria, and then the library. At each library, I could find the same books I had in the last school—the same familiar covers amongst the mob rotating strangers and new teachers.

In each new place, I would always checkout the same three books— renewing them every few weeks just so I could carry them around as comfort objects—something static in the chaos. The three books were a Peanuts story (the title of which I cannot recall), *My Side of the Mountain,* and a photography-rich travel book on the rugged landscape of Alaska. I was always transfixed by the images of the cavernous tunnels of blue ice and the silhouettes of gray wolves singing vapor into the chill air.

Eventually, my stepfather lost his life to an overdose when a batch of fentanyl-laced heroin was going around, and the need to move around stopped. However, the libraries remained a regular as I got older, and the challenges of life changed shape. My affection for books and words became a passion for writing and, eventually, for publishing.

LEFT: BACKCOUNTRY IN ABIQUIU, NM. CERRO PEDERNÁL IN THE DISTANCE. OCTOBER 2023 CONNOR WOLFE

Under my pen name, L.M. Browning, I've accomplished several career milestones. I founded two independent publishing houses; I gave a TEDx Talk at Yale; I earned a scholarship/grant to Harvard; I wrote fourteen books; I received five Pushcart Prize nominations; two Foreword Review Book Awards; the Nautilus Gold Medal for Poetry (2014); the Nautilus Silver Medal for Poetry (2022). As a publisher, I served two terms on the Board of the Independent Book Publisher's Association and have overseen the publication of over 300 titles.

In the autumn of 2022, when I changed my name and came out as nonbinary/trans, I disappeared into the high-desert of New Mexico to find enough space to hold all my feelings.

When I returned to the Northeast, colleagues and friends were pulling me aside at events—everyone asking, "When is the next book? I can't wait to hear how Connor Wolfe came to be…" This is a natural question, given that I have historically written intimately about my life experiences. Becoming Connor Wolfe would indeed be the story of my career. So why did I have no words to give to it?

It was over this past summer that I finally concluded that there would be no next book. I wasn't interested in writing. So now what? I'm a writer—I've built a 15-year career on this particular artistic expression. What the hell do I do now, just start over?

For a long time, I mistook not wanting to write for having nothing to say, but that wasn't true. I still wanted to capture story and character and place, but the language of that expression needed to evolve along with me.

I was walking through downtown Northampton—a haven for queer folk located in Western Massachusetts and the place I call home base. It was the first winter since I had come out as nonbinary/trans and changed my name, which also made it the first winter after both my mother

The entire social system imprinted on us from birth is a **colonization** *of our original* *wild self.*

and my father disowned me in the wake of that becoming. The cold was bone-deep that day. I was wrapped in my thick canvas chore coat and thermals. I ducked into my favorite shop (The Cedar Chest) to escape the frigid wind and look for a new journal for the new year. I was browsing through the well-curated stationery section when I passed by a small display of double-tipped markers and froze. The heaviness of words dissolved, and the timeworn wonderment of the spectrum of colors returned.

I didn't buy a new journal that afternoon. These days, I've traded Moleskins for sketchpads, my red pen for a plate knife, and books for photography (another artistic language of my youth).

LEFT: BACKCOUNTRY IN ABIQUIU, NM. GHOST RANCH OCTOBER 2023 CONNOR WOLFE

The shift from words back visual art was never done in a desire to end one career and begin another; just as my choice to take a new name was never meant to erase the person I was. I chose to return to visual art because I needed to evolve as an artist the way I was evolving as an individual—to follow the natural progression.

The desire to express myself through visual media seemed to be linked to the progression of my gender identity. As the *gender dysphoria* lifted, I was able to surface from my dissociative survival, come back into my body, integrate my emotions/memories, find the neglected child, see them, refuse to abandon them, and begin the process of reparenting myself. Somewhere in this larger process, old passions and youthful self-expressions returned with the fragments of suppressed self—among them, art.

Throughout my life, I've used different mediums to tell different parts of my journey. I communicated through my sketches and paintings to convey the unspoken and unspeakable. The publishing industry has always frowned on allowing the voice of the author to change—if you're going to change genres or tones—create a pen name, a new platform, a new persona for this new pursuit, and don't muddy the marketing waters. But when our business models and comfort zones have us cling to easy-to-market brands/personas, we rob ourselves of witnessing the evolution of the artist and by extension ourselves.

I set many intentions as I chose the name Connor Wolfe—one of which was the declaration to embrace the original wild self within me. The entire social system imprinted upon us from birth is a colonization of that original wild self. I reject this abusive dynamic and its systematic violence, choosing instead to live outside of that structure.

Needless to say, I am an unconventional person (and only becoming more so). I homestead in the warm months as I build up my off-grid farm in Western, Mass.—I hangout with slam poets, musicians, painters, activists, Buddhist monks, and refugees; spend my days with fellow queers, drag queens, and trans folk; I go to museums and hide in the back at open mics to hear the new voices...

Then, in the winter months, when I get shut out of the mountain, I roam—a modern-day cowboy vagabonding and boondocking my way through the backcountry of the still-wild places seeking awe to counterbalance the trauma burden I carry and to truly live my life close to the bone.

I spend time with the landscape. I postup with outliers and trade stories with subterraneans—those with no fixed home but deep roots—speaking in languages none of us have seen, or heard, or read—and these are the voices I hope to curate within these pages.

As I write this first letter from the editor under my chosen name, I invite the evolution of the artist, the magazine, the mediums, and indeed the individual as we endeavor to include all forms of storytelling, all viewpoints, and all experiences.

— *Connor Wolfe*

SHINRIN-YOKU AND THE FOREST-SPIRIT WAY

A REFLECTION ON FOREST MEDICINE, WAYFARING, AND BEYOND
BY EDITOR-AT-LARGE, *FRANK INZAN OWEN*

INTRODUCTION

Shinrin-yoku is a Japanese term first coined in 1982 by Tomohide Akiyama, the then Director General of the Japanese Ministry of Agriculture, Forestry, and Fisheries. The Japanese characters, or *kanji*, that form the word *shinrin-yoku* literally mean "forest bath". The term does not mean to take a literal bath in a forest. Instead, *shinrin-yoku* is a modern, poetic way of referring to a practice developed in contemporary times of *immersing oneself, fully, in the atmosphere of the forest* for purposes of mental and physical well-being. This sense of "bathing in the forest atmosphere" is a signature phrase of the *shinrin-yoku* and forest medicine movement. With a few notable exceptions, "forest bathing" (as a contemporary evolution) involves a brief experience in the forest, with an emphasis on the five senses and the various health benefits to the participant (e.g. stress-reduction).

In this essay, I want to briefly discuss *shinrin-yoku* and some of the scientific findings of forest medicine research. Then, I want to pivot to another consideration, namely, approaching the forest through an even wider aperture than the physical dimension alone.

Spending extended time in forests and mountains was a facet of my own studies and experiences with my late teacher, Darion Kuma Gracen (1949-2007), a wilderness guide, counselor-mentor, educator, amateur naturalist, and a Wayfarer of a unique, syncretic spiritual path. Her path wove together meditation practices from the Far East, methods of "dreaming-while-awake", a psychodynamic understanding of the soul (influenced by Jungian thought and Dreambody work developed by Arnold Mindell), and an animistic, experiential approach to Nature-connection (resonant with aspects of Japanese Shinto spirituality) that fosters a sense of the *numinous* (derived from the Latin: *numen*, arousing spiritual or religious emotion; mysterious or awe-inspiring stirrings; classically speaking, *numen*: spirit presiding over a thing or space, i.e. that which is perceived and experienced through means beyond the five senses). By including this numinous dimension to the experience of "immersing oneself, fully, in the atmosphere of the forest", we step into what Kuma-sensei called The Forest-Spirit Way. In the second part of this essay, I would like to explore some of these aspects.

"FOREST BATHING" AND FOREST MEDICINE: THE SCIENCE

Though the concept "forest bathing" may brush across the ear of some as merely a quaint notion, or may even strike some techno-addicted, Nature-avoidant city-dwellers as a downright odd-sounding pastime, the contemporary creation of *shinrin-yoku* – and the establishment of forest medicine research in general - initially arose as a direct response to two points of concern that Akiyama perceived as being dynamically interrelated; namely, a need to protect Japan's declining forests, and a way to address the increasing negative health effects he observed in urban Japanese people resulting from both work-stress and an obvious chronic disconnection from natural settings.

Though it will probably sound quite commonsensical to most readers of *Wayfarer Magazine* in the year 2023, back in the early 80s Akiyama's logic was visionary and culturally transformative:

If people can experience the health benefits of the forest they are much more likely to protect the forest.

This led to a robust campaign, with full backing of the Japanese government, funding a number of medical studies into the mental and physical health benefits of "taking in the forest atmosphere". Two of the primary individuals of note in the "shinrin-yoku lineage", who have been deeply involved in heading up this body of medical and psychological research, are Dr. Qing Li, author of *Forest Bathing: The Japanese Art and Science of Shinrin-Yoku* (subtitle: "How Trees Can Help You Find Health and Happiness") and Dr. Yoshifumi Miyazaki, author of *Shinrin Yoku: The Japanese Art of Forest Bathing*.

The medical and psychological studies that have been done on the various features of shinrin-yoku, naturally, are expressed in the parlance of science. Here are but a few examples from the dozens of studies that have been completed in the arena of forest medicine research:

- "Physiological Benefits of Viewing Nature: A Systematic Review of Indoor Experiments", H Jo, C Song, Y Miyazaki, *International Journal of Environmental Research and Public Health*, 2019

- "Physiological and Psychological Effects of Forest and Urban Sounds Using High-Resolution Sound Sources", H Jo, C Song, H Ikei, S Enomoto, H Kobayashi, Y Miyazaki

- *International Journal of Environmental Research and Public Health*, 2019

- "Sustained Effects of a Forest Therapy Program on the Blood Pressure of Office Workers",

- C Song, H Ikei, Y Miyazaki, *Journal of Urban Forestry & Urban Greening*, 2017

- "Physiological Effects of Nature Therapy: A Review of the Research in Japan", C Song, H Ikei, Y Miyazaki, *International Journal of Environmental Research and Public Health*, 2016

- "Effect of Forest Walking on Autonomic Nervous System Activity in Middle-Aged Hypertensive Individuals: A Pilot Study", C Song, H Ikei, M Kobayashi, T Miura, M Taue, T Kagawa, Q Li,

- *International Journal of Environmental Research and Public Health*, 2015

- "Physiological Effect of Olfactory Stimulation by Hinoki Cypress (*Chamaecyparis obtusa*) Leaf Oil", H Ikei, C Song, Y Miyazaki, *Journal of Physiological Anthropology*, 2015

- "The Physiological Effects of Shinrin-yoku (taking in the forest atmosphere or forest bathing): Evidence From Field Experiments in 24 Forests Across Japan", BJ Park, Y Tsunetsugu, T Kasetani, T Kagawa, Y Miyazaki, *Journal of Environmental Health and Preventive Medicine*, 2010

- "An Experimental Study on Physiological and Psychological Effects of Pine Scent", HJ Jo, E Fujii, TD Cho, *Journal of the Korean Institute of Landscape Architecture*, 2010

- "Phytoncides (wood essential oils) Induce Human Natural Killer Cell Activity", Q Li, A Nakadai, H Matsushima, Y Miyazaki, AM Krensky, T Kawada, *Journal of Immunopharmacology and Immunotoxicology*, 2006

Suddenly
I am hearing
my father's voice say:
"Break it down
for me, son.
What did they find?"

The forest is vital to human emotional/mental health and physical health.

The forest is, in fact, a source of preventative medicine, holistically.

Drs. Li, Miyazaki, Ikei, Jo, and others on their teams, have validated, resoundingly, what many of us already know intuitively:

Taking into account the primary foci of their research (including the multi-leveled effect of Nature imagery and Nature sounds on stress regulation — even when indoors, and the effect of what are called "terpenes" in the form of *phytoncides*, or essential oils of cedar, hinoki cypress, and pine) a few of the highlights from their collective findings is that **a *two-hour* session of forest bathing *once-per-month***:

- **significantly boosts the immune system (including cancer-fighting NK cells)**

- **improves concentration and memory (including with dementia)**

- **lowers cortisol (the stress hormone that leads to weight gain and heart disease)**

- **boosts serotonin and decreases both anxiety and depression**

- **reduces blood pressure**

- **drastically improves sleep**

- **lowers inflammation (resulting from breathing in terpenes and negative ions)**

The strong evidence of the mental and physical health benefits of *shinrin-yoku* ultimately led the Japanese government to designate natural areas (and whole forests) for the purpose of the study and practice of forest medicine. As of the writing of this article, there are over 10 dedicated "certified forest medicine bases" or "forest therapy centers" throughout Japan; and, the wide variance of forest bathing research being conducted isn't showing any signs of slowing down. So, the modern *shinrin-yoku* movement is alive, well, and spreading (like the roots of its original inspiration) to parts of Canada, Chile, Europe, Finland, and the U.S., where one major urban hospital in Atlanta launched a pilot program in forest bathing for cancer patients in collaboration with a local nature center.

Forest medicine has also influenced South Korea and Sweden (where forest bathing is called *samlim-yog* and *skogsbad*, respectively) to prioritize similar standards in research and investments in their citizenry and local ecology as has been done in Japan. According to Dr. Qing Li, Chairman of the Japanese Society for Forest Medicine, and Secretary-General of the International Society for Nature and Forest Medicine: "The South Korean government has spent more than $14 million on a National Forest Therapy Centre, has developed thirty-seven state-run recreational forests, and is training five hundred forest-healing instructors."

From influencing university studies, and how some psychotherapists work, to the creation of a whole new category of eco-tourism (where a guided forest bathing session can be booked from the comfort of your hotel room or bungalow), the *shinrin-yoku* movement has branched outward from its initial seed-concept in Japan into a diversity of applications, approaches, books, international training programs, and applied forms of what is now called "forest therapy". (see *Resources* below)

Certainly, I am a celebrant of *most* of this. I've personally benefited from the forest medicine research that has taken place and support the research that continues. I am thoroughly convinced that—in the years to come – medical science (through the efforts of forest medicine research) will so clearly prove and convey the vital necessity for humans to be consciously bonded to healthy, thriving landscapes that it will have even deeper impacts, globally, on government priorities, including boosting the discipline of Nature-centric city planning.

That said, as I reflect on my own experiences of connecting deeply with forests, I have to acknowledge that something equally vital is being left out in the overtly scientific approach; something equally as important, equally as present as the invisible forest *phytoncides* that are of such benefit to our immune systems. I would like to attempt to talk about these features by returning to the signature phrase of the forest medicine movement itself: *immersing oneself, fully, in the atmosphere of the forest.*

DREAMING WITH THE FOREST: THE FOREST-SPIRIT WAY

"The Universe is our greatest teacher, our greatest friend. It is always teaching us the Art of Peace.
Study how the water flows in a valley stream, smoothly and freely between the rocks.
Everything—mountains, rivers, plants, and trees – should be your teacher."

– O Sensei, Morihei Ueshiba (1883-1969), Founder of Aikidō

When I think of my own relationship to forests, it often presents itself in the form of memories—memories stored in cells. Memories connected to bare footfalls through sandy creek beds and boot-laced feet moving over rocks and through underbrush. Memories of trails and switchbacks. Memories of bucks stomping ground, coyotes howling, hawks and crows calling from above. Memories of napping in hollows filled with such a cushion of pine needles,...to this day I have yet to sleep as deeply (or been able to find a mattress that approaches the same level of comfort). The earliest memories involve childhood. Time for a poem.

"Little Cowboy, Stumbling"

jumping into mounds of leaves
napping like a deer in pine hollows
breathing deep of the incense
of butterscotch pines

discovering abandoned shells
of cicadas left clinging to a Loblolly

hours observing tadpoles in a woodland pool

sheer delight from "forest-stumbling" —
stumbling upon a hawk feather
stumbling upon a deer skull
stumbling upon a coiled kingsnake

sunrise
pine-wind
sunset
moonrise
tree frogs
cricket-song

how could I have known, back then,
that *this* would become my religion?

Later on in time, I would encounter *one* of the deep teachers of my path: Kuma-sensei (to me), "doña Río" (to some) — a rascally ol' "tumbleweed" with ancestors like mine – back to Scandinavia, rural England, and Scotland. When I think of her now, a strange, dreamy, archetypal image arises in my awareness: a cross between a cloaked *völva* (Norse wisewoman), or perhaps a Druid priestess, and a female *yamabushi* (Japanese mountain-priest ascetic). With a penchant for laughter, word-play, tawny port wine, and New Mexican green chiles, my predominant memory of her is of long stretches of piñon-wind *zazen* (meditation) under the moon.

Though I spent many an hour wandering through forests as a young man (even skipping high school graduation to consciously mark that "rite of passage" by sitting on "my rock" deep in a North Carolina wood), it wasn't until I crossed paths with Kuma-sensei that I realized much more fully that Nature is my religion.

> "I believe in God, only I spell it Nature."
> — Frank Lloyd Wright, Nature-inspired architect

This declaration isn't an overlay, an add-on, or something lifted from some other place. It's home-grown, cultivated from the heart-mind and soul, but it is cross-cultural. If we go back far enough in any of our ancestral lines, it is universal: Nature-as-sacred presence. All of us hail from people who originally experienced Nature as a numinous reality. Wayfarers in every culture have spoken of mountains as teachers, the forest as a healer. Nature was the original spirituality. Yet, this quality of consciousness and reverence isn't a level of perception, engagement, or experience that is usually passed on consciously from generation to generation in our modern context. It is an attribute that must be cultivated from within and it is an attribute greatly needed in the here and now.

In the words of Motohisa Yamakage, a 79th generation Shinto priest, author of *The Essence of Shinto*: "Shinto teaches to revere Great Nature. Nature is the transformation and creation of *Kami,* therefore the sacredness of *Kami* dwells within it...The Japanese people have loved and revered Nature as a gift from Kami since ancient times. We have felt that plants and animals, as well as mountains and rivers, have lived with us and have been deeply connected to us. This love and reverence toward Nature is a quality that should be reinstalled in our hearts, if we want humankind and earth to survive the ecological crisis that has resulted from excessive materialism."

Great Nature (大自然, *Daishizen* in Japanese) wasn't initially a focus of the dialogue with my teacher. It was an ever-present backdrop, but it wasn't something articulated until later. Over time, however, it became clear that everything I was studying with her — different forms of meditation, methods of *dreaming-while-awake*, sacred inquiry, contemplative poetics, time spent in forests (and even caves for brief "dark retreats") — all existed to facilitate a dual process; a gradual purification, on the one hand, and greater alignment on the other. The purification was a purification of perception; from the inherited Western-enculturated, conditioned-masculine, and the burdened, encumbered "lower-self". The alignment was one of coming into deeper and deeper levels of connection to Great Nature.

Kuma-sensei's thoughts on Great Nature can best be summed up with a few key phrases:

- Great Nature is a power we can never fully comprehend

- We can live in or out of essential alignment with Great Nature; meditation, time in Nature, methods of dreaming or purification methods (like a sauna or misogi, a mental-physical-spiritual purification practice undertaken beneath an ice-cold waterfall) can restore our connection through the somatic doorway of the body

- Great Nature is sentient, intelligent, and wise in terms of dynamic energy, sustaining power, and prevalent patterns (symbolized in the dynamic movement in both the ancient symbol known as the mitsudomoe used in Shinto and the Tai Ji /yin-yang in Taoism)

- There is a numinous, spiritual dimension to Great Nature that can be transformative for humans

- The numinous dimension of Great Nature is restorative to the soul (just as forest medicine can be healing to body and mind through phytoncides, Nature imagery, Nature sounds, and slower rhythms)

- We can connect with this numinous dimension of Great Nature because we, too, are part of Great Nature (Shinto tradition says we are children of Kami, thus children of Great Nature; in the Nature writings of C.G. Jung, he speaks of our own psyche being comprised of the same numinous essence as Nature)

We can connect with Great Nature via the five senses but we can also commune, connect, and communicate with Great Nature in ways that are beyond the five senses (and the intellect) through experiences that involve different forms of attention, intuitive perception, and dreaming (an interesting side note: one word in Japanese for dream-visioning is *musō* (夢想), part of which is constructed of a kanji that combines the radicals for 'heart-mind and spirit' (心), 'eye' (目), and 'tree' (木); it offers something of a practice-hint: to connect with the deeper dream (夢), we can go into the trees (木) to look (目) with our heart-mind-spirit (心)

Additional concepts from Shinto tradition can assist us in comprehending the Japanese understanding of a numinous approach to Nature. These concepts are *tama* (魂 "soul" or "spirit" 霊) and *kokoro* (心). *Tama* isn't just a word but is something that is experienced, viscerally and intuitively. *Tama* is felt, known, and perceived. It is an early Shinto term for spiritual power; a specific type of vital power that is awe-inspiring and leads to a profound sense of connectedness.

Running like an underground river beneath and through all of Japanese spirituality is *kokoro* ("heart-mind"; or, in the words of Thomas Kasulis, author of *SHINTO: The Way Home*, another teacher of mine in all things Shinto, *kokoro* means a "mindful-heart"). This term derives from the term *makoto no kokoro* – a pure heart of sincerity. Rather than heart-as-object or heart-as-noun (as in the physical heart beating in our chest), *kokoro* is heart-as-verb, heart-as-energy field that connects with the world in an engaged and responsive way.

Shinto spiritual praxis, in part, consists of connecting with Great Nature at sites known to be *kami*-filled and *tama*-charged. A person brings their *kokoro* (their mindful-heart) into alignment with the spirit of place and this produces a shift in consciousness. The Japanese landscape is filled with markers (such as *torii* gates, special walkways, and forest shrines) that remind people of the presence of *kami* and act as holographic entry points for people to experience a reconnection to the numinous. In the words of T.P. Kasulis, "*Kokoro* is cognition with affect, affect with cognition… To experience the extraordinary, one has to be open to being affectively touched by the phenomenon and its *tama*."

Part and parcel of my experiences with Kuma was approaching the realm of Great Nature (usually forests and mountains but also, at times, deserts and arroyos) by employing such expanded senses, what Zurich-trained Jungian analyst Arnold Mindell calls "the dreambody", and what I have grown to think of as the faculty of *soft-attention* (a loose, flowing, receptive quality of multi-sensory awareness rather than the hyper-focused concentration emphasized by modernity).

In Mindell's own words:

> *"The dreambody is a multi-channeled information sender asking you to receive its message in many ways and noticing how its information appears over and over again… The dreambody is your wise signaller, giving you messages in many different dimensions. When it signals to you in the body, we call it a symptom or sensation. When it signals to you through a dream, we call it a symbol."*

With these multidimensional senses "along for the ride", so to speak, sometimes Kuma and I explored the visual contours of mountains and rolling forested landscapes as flute-songs (offerings of spontaneous tunes to Nature on different kinds of flutes, matching the notes to the rise and fall of the horizon line). We frequently explored day-long sessions of hillwalking and forest-walking as an unfurling process of poem-making, sometimes "stalking poems" like a hunter or birdwatcher, or — once we had connected energetically with the spirit of place — expressing what emerged for us (or what was made known to us) by communing with a certain locale.

Eventually, like sunlight filtering down through pine tassels and juniper bows, Kuma began more consciously connecting some dots for me, making me aware that all we had been doing — which she called *Wayfaring* at times, and *The Forest-Spirit Way* at other times — hadn't been sourced wholly with her but rather was an approach resonant with and influenced by more ancient ways-within-the-Way (such as Shinto, Daoism, Shugendō, the Way of Tea, and the mountains-and-forests Zen of so many Wayfarers and hermit-poets).

We didn't speak of *phytoncides* or "forest bathing". The results of the medical research studies cited previously weren't known at the time. Yet, the deep psychospiritual, soul-transforming benefits of time in the forest was intimately known. In the presence of the Forest-Spirit, wounds were healed. In the embrace of Great Nature, old traumas were transmuted. We spoke of *kami*, the spirit of certain mountains and forests, and of poets who had a deep love affair with forests like Rengetsu (1791-1875) and Saigyō (1118-1190), Bashō (1644-1694) and Santōka (1882-1940), Oliver (1935-2019), Snyder (1930-   ), and Berry (1957-   ); and, like other hermit-poets—who would sometimes wander into the mountains and forests, or who would sit for days in silence, gazing at mountains from their solitary hut—this became our practice-focus as well.

At the end of her life, she said I would have to find my own way of *Wayfaring*, my own way of walking the *Forest-Spirit Way*. "It won't be my way exactly. It won't be someone else's way. If it's someone else's way, it won't be your way. Great Nature is the teacher." Time for another poem.

"Amerikua Shinrinbushi"

slow rhythm

silence

the soul unfurls

the poet's dreamingbody

stretches out

to the horizon

realizes itself inseparable

from the dreambody

of Great Nature's light

the instructions come

from the Forest-Spirit Way:

sit like a mountain

breathe like a forest

flow like a river

BEING HELD BY EARTH: FOREST HEALING AFTER CANCER

When I think of healing and connecting with sacred forests, I can't help but think of my own mother, Dale. Diagnosed with breast cancer nearly a decade ago, she retired from her role as a trainer of chaplains due to the gradual impact of her treatments. For the first year, after her single mastectomy and radiation, she could hardly move due to fatigue. From the outside looking in, it seemed as if she had entered a deep sleep that hovered in the borderlands of choice. Would her spirit stay, or would her spirit go?

Then, one day, she arose from the couch and for the next year spent hours upon hours among the many trees and foliage that make up the wooded half-acre behind her home. It is a serene place filled with Japanese lanterns, quiet sitting places, and a multitude of trees, both old growth poplars and grandmother pines as well as new arrivals — dogwoods, sakura, Japanese maples, azaleas and fern, Gold Dust (*Aucuba japonica*) and Heavenly Bamboo (*Nandina domestica*).

Of that time, she speaks of taking up the task of "working with the trees", apprenticing to them, getting her hands into the soil, asking the trees what they wanted. Their collaboration was a co-tending.

She states:

I began noticing all of the life — the birds, the chipmunks, the squirrels; all the little creatures going on about their business, doing their little chores. Then I started noticing all of the plants and the trees. I realized I needed to get closer. I wanted to know all of these presences more intimately. So, I began to work in the yard, a little bit at a time. There's a big hill that drops down like a terrace and it was all covered over with debris, so I started clearing some of that away, over time, and revealing what was underneath. Huge rocks, plants, trees that couldn't reach the sunlight.

It felt as if I was stroking the face of the Earth, and there were things underneath all of that debris that needed to have things taken out of their face. They were under a foot of leaves. Some leaves are fine but this was choking the life out of everything, so I started inching my way across this hill, and I felt like I was in a dance with the forest. It was very moving.

In time, I felt like I could just let go. I could curl up and be held by the land and be healed. I stayed out there for a year doing that. Nobody told me to go out and lay down on the hill. I just knew I needed to do it. It was a very natural, intuitive process that — as a creature, along with all the other creatures — I instinctively knew what I needed to do. It wasn't a mental thing. It was a heart thing. It was a gut thing. It was a visceral feeling. I needed to be close to the Earth. I needed to embrace the plants. If I could have held every creature, I would have had them all over me, and allowed them to teach me their lessons.

I've learned some of those lessons, from afar, as I've watched them dig for food and bury their acorns for the Fall. They're just like us. We're just like they are. There is no true separation. If you can understand that, you will never treat the Earth poorly, and you will help heal Her."

I'm reminded of the words of Tim Ryosen Bunting, a New Zealander now living in Japan, who was initiated into the Dewa Sanzan tradition of Shugendō - the Way of Yamabushidō. In a recent dialogue he said:

Forests are part of Nature. For yamabushi, Nature is the womb.
Nature is all-knowing and it is where we absorb the lessons of life.

Undoubtedly, Great Nature has been a womb of rebirth for my mother.
I have seen it with my own eyes. The same can be true for any of us,
whether we approach Nature as a forest bathing exercise, or as a
multidimensional spiritual practice. *Immersing oneself, fully, in the forest
atmosphere* isn't something new. It forms the bedrock of the most ancient
form of spirituality for the Japanese people (and continues to influence
consciousness despite modernization). Likewise, the Wayfarers of old
(along with all our ancestors) knew that Nature heals, imparts teachings,
and has the capacity to initiate us into greater levels of awareness.

As much as I appreciate the modern *shinrin-yoku* movement, and the
general scientific inquiry of forest medicine as an arena of research, it
feels equally important to me to consider the numinous dimensions and
implications of connecting with Great Nature. It seems a good thing to ask
from time to time when *immersing oneself, fully, in the forest atmosphere*:
What exactly do we mean by "immersing...fully"? Are we aware of all that
inhabits the "forest atmosphere"? What exactly do we mean by "oneself"?

May the Forest Be With You

FRANK INZAN OWEN HE/HIM is a solitary Wayfarer of a Nature-oriented
contemplative and creative path inspired by Japanese spiritual
principles. He is the author of three books of poetry with Homebound
Publications and curates the podcast The Poet's Dreamingbody.

RESOURCES

Apps

One of the interesting findings of not only the forest medicine research group in Japan but also the Acoustical Society of America ("Natural Sounds Improve Mood and Productivity", from a 2015 study) is that even sitting indoors listening to the sounds of Nature (such as while working) assists with lowering stress, increasing focus, and elevating positive feelings. A few of the apps (available on both Android and in the Apple Store) that have sounds of water, rain, waves, crickets, cicadas, wind blowing through a bamboo grove or forest, and more, include:

- **myNoise** (free with additional fee for expanded recordings)
- **NatureSpace** (free with additional fee for expanded recordings)
- **Aura** (subscription based)
- **Calm** (subscription based)

Training Programs

- The Association of Nature and Forest Therapy Guides and Programs
  www.natureandforesttherapy.org *(*based in the U.S.)*

- The Mindful Tourist Shinrin-Yoku Certification Training
  www.themindfultourist.net *(*based in Thailand and Japan with branches in Brazil, Mexico, Singapore, and Sweden)*

- Yamabushido: Transformative Yamabushi Training
  www.yamabushido.jp *(*based in Yamagata, Japan)*

Forest Medicine Research Websites

- Forest Medicine Therapy Society in Japan
  www.fo-society.jp

- The Society for Forest Medicine in Japan
  www.forest-medicine.com

- International Society of Nature and Forest Medicine
  www.inform.org

-

Books (and Audiobooks)

- *Your Guide To Forest Bathing*
  by M. Amos Clifford

    *(*There are a plethora of books coming out about forest bathing but this is the first I have seen that incorporates the 'more than the five senses' approach through a variety of practices Clifford categorizes as imaginal, heart sense, proprioception, and body radar)*

- *The Holotropic Mind*
  by Stanislav Grof, M.D. with Hal Zina Bennett

- *China Root: Taoism, Ch'an, and Original Zen*
  by David Hinton

- *Hunger Mountain: A Field Guide to Mind and Landscape*
  by David Hinton

- *Forest Medicine*
  by Qing Li

- *Forest Bathing: The Japanese Art and Science of Shinrin-Yoku*
  by Dr. Qing Li

- *Your Brain on Nature*
  by Alan Logan and Eva Selhub

- *The Shaman's Body: A New Shamanism for Transforming Health, Relationships, and the Community*
  by Arnold Mindell

- *Working With The Dreaming Body*
  by Arnold Mindell

- *Shinrin-Yoku: The Japanese Way of Forest Bathing*
  by Yoshifumi Miyazaki

- *The Earth Has A Soul: The Nature Writings of C.G. Jung*
  edited by Meredith Sabini

- *Sight and Sensibility: The Ecopsychology of Perception*
  by Laura Sewell

- *The Nature Fix*
  by Florence Williams

- *The Art of Peace by Morihei Ueshiba*
  (translated and edited by John Stevens)

- *The Essence of Shinto: Japan's Spiritual Heart*
  by Motohisa Yamakage

COWBOY BOOTS AND PONYTAILS

BY EDITOR-AT-LARGE, KRISTEN WILLIAMS

A Reflection on L. M. Browning's Conversation with Frank Inzan Owen *Far Rider: Field Notes on Gender Identity, Facing Intergenerational Trauma, and Seeking Awe in the High Desert*

My reading of L. M. Browning's interview about the journey of gender identity and expression brought up so many thoughts for me regarding my own experience of gender identity/expression, and also regarding the psyche's experience of genderedness that I have come to understand, believe in, and resonate with as an adult and a helping professional.

I was born and still identify as female. I also grew up a tomboy. I experienced some childhood perception that this was considered slightly irregular by my family, but I'm thankful that it wasn't completely quashed in the permissiveness of my existence as a child—because I've come to understand that it could've been. Don't get me wrong—my mother and I went rounds about appropriate dress for church...keyword being *dress*. I hated dresses as a child and was mostly obliged that preference; the exceptions being school picture day and Sunday church. I remember one particular Sunday when this weekly battle came to a head. My mother, in exasperation, spat out, "Well what is it you *want* to wear?" Moments later I emerged from my bedroom wearing a white t-shirt with my name ironed on in simple black letters across the chest—the iron-on letters having been a gift from the bottom of the cereal box—red and white striped shorts, and cowboy boots. I remember being very proud of my ensemble. I was four. Needless to say, I didn't win that battle—I ended up pouting in the pew wearing a dress of which I have no specific memory. But I do remember so very many more moments of joy in my childhood wearing boots and capes and wielding swords, knives, and bows and arrows.

I wasn't exclusively tomboy, however. In addition to Robin Hood, I was also Laura Ingalls in my woods play. I played with Barbies, *Star Wars* figures, and Adventure People. Adventure People were the same size figures as the *Star Wars* characters but were designed for camping and hiking situations. They came with a jeep and a tent and a canoe, and the girl figure was outfitted in denim shorts, button-up shirt, hiking boots, and a ponytail. Truth be told, my Han Solo was more into Adventure girl than he was Princess Leia in my crossover action-figure world. Furthermore, when my friends played make-believe, I was usually (and willingly) cast as the boy character in the given make-believe scene. Somebody had to be the boy, apparently it made sense to everybody for it to be me.

But I also remember praying a prayer of thanks one day to have been born a girl. It wasn't because I thought boys were gross or mean as little girls often do; rather,

I was about six and this thanksgiving occurred to me specifically because it made me happy to get to wear a ponytail. Clearly, no boy I knew was allowed to have hair long enough for a ponytail in my south Mississippi town of only 2400 souls.

I recall that I never thought I should have been a boy, and yet I also felt so very comfortable inhabiting masculine gender stereotypical ways of being. As I grew into my teenage years, I still felt more comfortable in jeans and t-shirts, even though I was well aware that the boys with whom I was smitten were choosing to pay attention to the girly girls with bows in their hair and cute little outfits. Somewhere along the way in early high school I struck a semi-conscious compromise with myself—I curled my hair and wore minimal makeup and stuck with the jeans and t-shirts. Dressing up still felt like putting on a costume, which only seemed fun on an occasion like prom, sort of the same way Halloween makes you feel game to wear crazy things you otherwise would not. But truth be told, putting on a dress and heels any other day of the year would have made me feel like an impostor. Conditioned by my upbringing, I only wore dresses to church and other mandatory dress up occasions like weddings, awards day, and graduation.

This preference for and comfort with more masculine-casual wear continued through college and grad school with only minor exceptions such as a purple suede mini skirt that I truly loved. Mostly because it was purple.

I entered into my early professional life in a male dominated vocation that valued conservative frumpiness in women, so my jeans turned to slacks and a love of clunky leather shoes interspersed with loose-fitting, long conventional skirts and mousy dresses. Anything that would remotely fall into the category of sexy still felt synonymous with impostor.

It wasn't until I went through the transformative crisis of divorce that I began to dabble in that costume world of girl clothes. I can honestly say this bit of play was not at all motivated by a desire to attract a new spouse; rather, it was entirely a matter of identity exploration and a desire to connect with parts of self that felt foreign to me. If everything I had understood and taken for granted was falling apart, I might as well turn on all the internal lights and see what else is in there. It felt awkward at first, and then gradually shifted into a feeling of daring and power, which is a little ironic given that external reactions to my increasingly feminized wardrobe were completely unexceptional. What felt new and different to me appeared to the outside world simply as the expected uniform. I must confess, I quickly discovered a liking for heels—after learning to walk in them—because I am 5'2" and the height boost was sensationally empowering.

It is sheer coincidence that my venturing into the land of stereotypical femininity traveled more or less alongside my vocational movement from local church ministry to psychotherapy. And as I followed my theoretical therapeutic instincts into the landscape of Jungian psychology, I was introduced to a foundational Jungian concept that began to make my gendered life make sense—that of *anima* and *animus*. Anima and Animus is Latin for soul, and they are gendered feminine and masculine respectively. In classical Jungian thought, anima and animus fulfill a compensatory function in the psyche. To put it most simply, Jung asserted that biological males possess an anima—a feminine internal aspect, and conversely biological females possess an animus—a masculine internal aspect. Many modern Jungian thinkers, however, perceive anima and animus as existing together in all persons regardless of anatomy or gender identity and expression, in other words, all persons possess both. Furthermore, anima and animus are understood more as energies within the psyche rather than culturally scripted behavior or personality structures. Animus is an outward flowing energy, while anima is an inward flowing energy. For example, the energy of aggression would be attributed to animus, the energy of connection to anima. This watershed bit of learning on my part made my childhood—and then my late thirties—both make sense.

I now believe that I was very conscious of my animus energy as a child. And while I could spend another whole dissertation-length reflection on what conspired within and without to awaken a more conscious awareness and appreciation of my anima energy, I will simply say that anima showed up in a more compelling way for me at that point in my life. So which one is the real me? Have I grown into my true self—my feminine self, or was my tomboy self my true self? The answer is yes. Both are fully me, and the goal of my healthy self-expression and understanding at this point is to honor whichever happens to be showing up in a given moment or season of my life. In fact, the goal of the Jungian journey of individuation is to integrate all the psyche's diverse parts toward an end of welcoming a beautifully colorful and non-homogenous wholeness.

I've been asked when trying to articulate this understanding, does that mean I do not believe that transgender is real? In other words, if one's gender identity and/or expression is a function of anima and animus energy, does that mean a transgender person is not really experiencing a misalignment between cultural expectations of body and soul but instead just has a greater expression of one or the other? On the contrary, I believe the transgender experience is 100% real. I've listened deeply to the painfully self-estranged experiences of transgender persons, and they are not the same as my experience growing up a tomboy. I'm a cis-gender female who deeply experienced my inner masculinity as more comfortable to me than my femininity in my younger years. And yet I never felt that I was [supposed to be] a boy. I experienced an atypical comfort with opposite gender self-expression; transgender persons are truly living with a misalignment between anatomy and selfhood.

I appreciated the inclusion of a glossary of terms in the midst of the interview, as it's also quite true that the experience of gender is not as simple as cis or trans. My own experience and the understanding of anima and animus help me to understand new gender identity parlance such as gender non-binary, gender non-conforming, and gender fluid. It has also helped me to become conscious of many gender stereotypes in which my culture brought me up and realize the meaning that became attached to many gendered notions in my young psyche that needs separating out and in some cases redefining. For example, my childhood masculine energy felt like strength, confidence, being taken seriously. Was this the culture's teaching? Or was this just a comfortable and healthy place inside my own being that I somehow already knew to value early on? I would say yes to both. Externally, culture attributes confidence and agency to masculinity, and as a child I appropriated that self-expression in my dress and play. Internally, my animus energy was strong and vibrant, and thankfully, felt authentic to me. It was only in my late thirties and into my forties that I experienced femininity as strong and authentically possessing power and agency. The fact that I had to learn this truth late in life and by means of intentionality and exploration is also an unfortunate product of the gender stereotypes in which I was formed. But just like femininity does not have ownership of Barbies and dresses, masculinity does not own strength, confidence, and credibility. We simply cannot drop every personality trait, preference, or inclination into one of two gender boxes and go on our way expecting all the world to conform to these supposed agreements.

That said, I wonder if concepts like gender fluid or gender non-binary are just another way of expressing the healthy integration of anima and animus into one's conscious self-perception. Another fundamental Jungian concept is that of

holding the tension of opposites. Jung believed that if one could cease the internal tug-of-war between two opposing ideas or compulsions and instead simply hold the two opposing notions as both valid and true, then a new third and transcendent understanding would arise out of the midst of that generative tension. In other words, rather than staying stuck in the psychic competition of male vs. female, perhaps making space for anima and animus to cohabit the soul together creates a new healthy and integrated *whole person*. One who can play with Barbies and swords. One who can wear high heels and drive a truck. One who can show up to decorate the church on the day before her wedding wearing a bride t-shirt, ripped jeans, and mud boots.

My corner of the Wayfarer tapestry is that of community. How is this reflection on gender about community, one might ask? Because community is nourished by diversity. And relationship with other grows in the fertile ground of comfort with difference. Community does not fit into our dichotomous boxes. Community does not merely tolerate perceived otherness, it celebrates it and is curious to get to know it. Community makes a place at the table for experiences that are different from mine, and then lingers over second helpings and dessert crumbs to hear more of the story. Community foregoes the need to quickly define things as good or bad, right or wrong, this or that, and instead says, "Tell me about it." And then the really sweet spot is when we find resonance in the midst of differing stories, as I did in listening to the soul-sharing of L.M. Browning/Connor L. Wolfe.

FAR RIDER

The Final Interview with Poet L. M. Browning

In Conversation with Frank 'Frozen' Owen, Editor-at-Large
with photography from Taos, New Mexico by Connor L. Wolfe

KRISTEN WILLIAMS SHE/HER is a licensed professional counselor and possesses a PhD in Depth Psychology with emphasis in Jungian and Archetypal Studies. She's also a foodie, a music lover, a public radio nerd, and has a passion for community and relationship building.

T

IS FOR

TOKITAE

BY EDITOR-AT-LARGE, IRIS GRAVILLE

AN ALPHABETICAL HOMAGE
TO THE ENDANGERED
SOUTHERN RESIDENT
KILLER WHALES

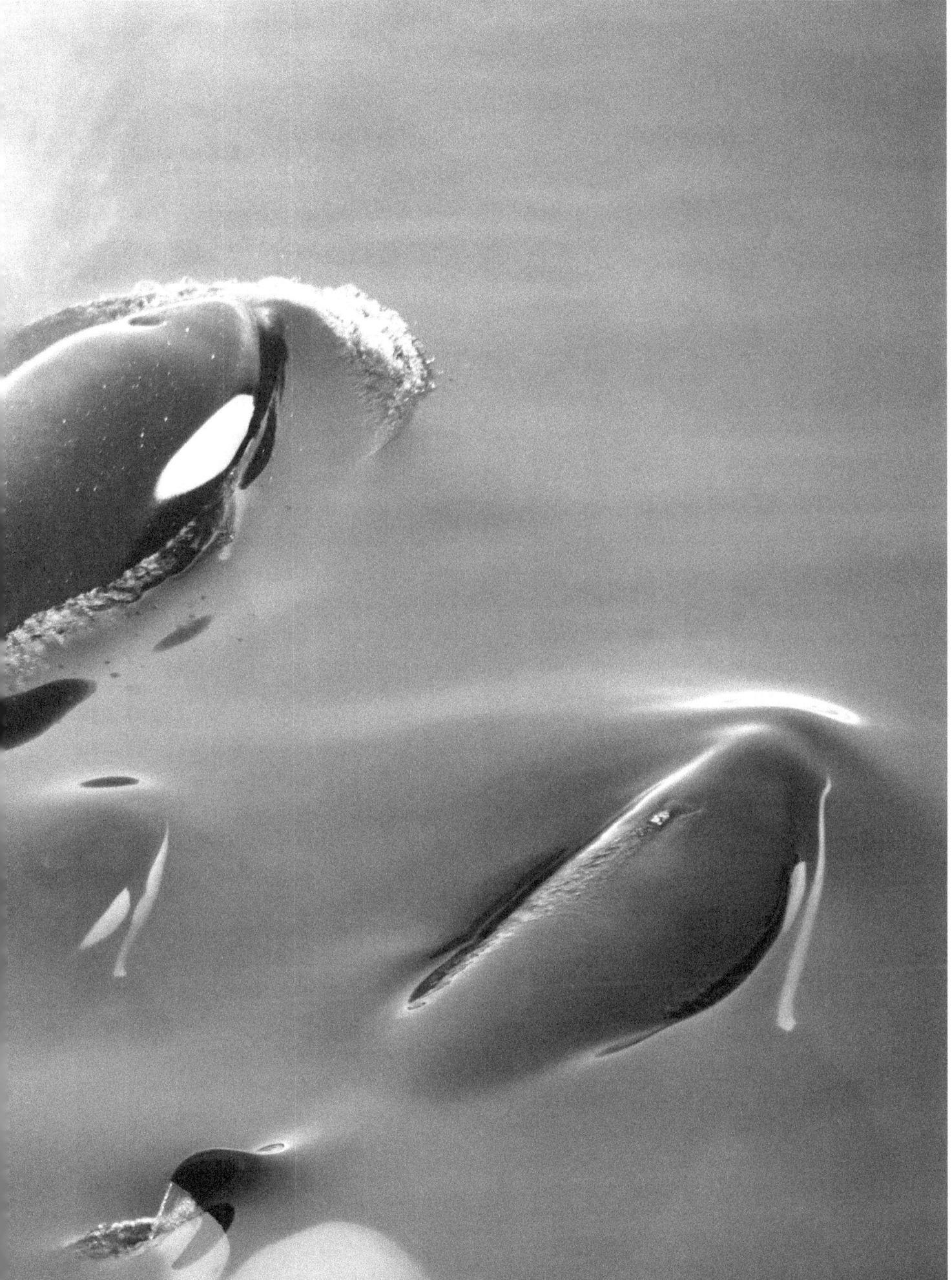

is for age.

Male orca whales (bulls) tend to live into their forties, but sometimes up to fifty years. Females (cows) typically live into their eighties. Cows reach reproductive maturity between the ages of thirteen and fifteen. Bulls begin breeding around age twenty-five. Calves are weaned after turning one.

B is for breathing.

Unlike humans, killer whales are voluntary breathers—they have to consciously remember to take a breath every time they need air. They breathe through a blowhole on the top of their heads, similar to the nostril in other mammals. When closed, the blowhole is completely airtight; to take a breath, muscles contract to open the blowhole's flap. This means orcas can't sleep the same way humans do, or they would drown (**see Z is for zzzz -sleeping**).

B is also for brain.

Orca whales have the second-largest brain of any animal. A mature orca brain weighs between twelve and fifteen pounds. The average human brain weighs nine pounds.

C is for Chinook salmon,

the red and silver-toned fish that make up about eighty percent of the Southern Resident orca diet. Chinook (also known as kings) are the largest and fattiest of all the Pacific salmon, thus are a good source of calories for the extremely active Southern Residents. They hatch in freshwater streams, then make their way hundreds of miles to the ocean to enrich their bodies with carbon and nitrogen. Chinooks (as well as other salmon) spend years in the ocean before finding their way back to the rivers where they were born to mate, lay eggs, and die. The nutrients their bodies carry back upriver become important food and fertilizer for land and river ecosystems, helping everything from trees to birds to bears. Chinooks are shrinking in size, however. In the early 1900s, they typically weighed around sixty pounds and sometimes as much as one hundred pounds; today, their average weight is closer to thirty pounds.

D is for dams.

Wild Pacific salmon spend most of their lives in the Pacific Ocean, but freshwater rivers and streams are where their lives begin and end. The Columbia River Basin in the Pacific Northwest was once among the greatest salmon-producing river systems in the world, likely responsible for over half the Chinook salmon in the range of Southern Resident orcas. In the 1960s, the Government built four hydroelectric dams on the lower Snake River in Washington, blocking more than half of salmon spawning and rearing habitat access. In 2000, the Government acknowledged that removing these dams would help recover endangered salmon and whales. But in July 2020, the Trump administration announced the Lower Snake dams would not be removed.

Previous dam removals around the country have been successful at aiding fish recovery and river restoration. In fact, Western Washington saw the largest dam removal thus far in the country with the demolition of two dams on the Elwha River in 2011 and 2014. The project opened seventy miles of habitat that had been blocked for a century. Scientists are seeing all five species of salmon native to the river, including Chinook, coming back.

E is for echolocation,

the sixth sense of orcas. They talk to each other and hunt by producing clicks, whistles, and pulsed calls transmitted through the melon—fatty tissue in the whale's forehead. This produces a directional and amplified sound that travels in water up to 800 meters. Those sound waves bounce back to the orcas in the form of echoes, received by the lower jaw, then through the auditory nerve to the brain, thus helping them detect where objects and other orcas are in the area.

Through this sense, orcas not only see the shape of the object, they can also see inside it. Like a submarine using sonar, or an obstetrician with a sonogram, orcas are able to send out pulses of sound that relay information to create a visual picture. This sophisticated technique detects the difference between species of salmon, so orcas can expend their energy into catching the fatty Chinook (see **C is for Chinook salmon**). Each pod possesses a unique set of calls, learned and culturally transmitted among individuals, that maintain group cohesion and serve as family badges.

F is for fin. Whales generally have four fins: two pectoral fins (instead of arms), a caudal fin (the tail), and a dorsal fin. Pectoral fins, just behind the head, are paddle-shaped and used for steering, turning, and stopping. Nerves inside the pectoral fins help regulate body temperature. The powerful muscles of the caudal fin move up and down for propulsion. The dorsal fin acts like the keel of a boat, keeping the whale from rolling side to side while swimming.

G is for Granny (J2). Believed to be born in 1911, Granny died in 2016. She's probably the world's longest-living Southern Resident orca. Many think of her as the symbol of the matriarchy defining the social structure of killer whales.

H is for health. The health of Southern Residents is threatened by multiple causes, including pollution, inadequate food, and boat disturbance and noise that make it harder for them to hunt. **H is also for heartbreaking.** With every death of a Southern Resident, people worry that the species will become extinct. "Heartbroken" was the word used repeatedly at the news in August 2023 of the death of the last Southern Resident in captivity (see **T is for Tokitae**).

I is for identify. Sparked by the increase in live capture for aquaria and public concern, scientists have been studying resident pods along the northern Pacific coast of the United States and Canada since 1970. By 1973, photographs were being used to identify individuals based on differences in saddle color pattern, dorsal fin shapes, and other identifying marks and scars. Identified orcas have all been numbered, and scientists keep careful records of their re-sightings.

J is for J pod. K is for K pod. L is for L pod. The Southern Resident killer whale community is formed of three pods (groups) known as J, K and L. Orcas generally live in pods consisting of several females, calves, several males, and/or juveniles. Some pods consist of a mother and her offspring, who stay with her for life. This matrilineal family structure has been observed in the Pacific Northwest, where resident pods have been documented as stable, consistent family groups with several generations traveling together. Each pod has its own dialect, but they also share a set of calls so that when they come together, they can communicate, socialize and mate.

The pod letters were first assigned to the two communities of fish-eating killer whales in the 1970s and were based on observed family relationships and association between the families and their unique dialects and vocalizations. The letters denote the pod of the mother's family. The Northern Resident community of orca pods use the letters A to I. The smaller community of Southern Resident whales are denoted by the letters J, K, and L. While researchers love numbers, non-scientists prefer names. So, the Whale Museum in Friday Harbor, Washington, asks its members to vote for a name for new calves of the year. Usually, the calf name will have some association with the mother. For example, the son of Eclipse was named Nova, to keep the celestial theme.

According to the Center for Whale Research, as of July 2022, J pod had twenty-five members, K pod had sixteen, and L pod had thirty-two, for a total population of seventy-three.

M is for mammal. Orca whales live in the ocean, but they're not fish. They are mammals.

N is for noise. Orcas change their behavior when vessels come closer than 400 yards. Females will either not initiate foraging dives or stop foraging if they are. Males are more typically seen in deeper water, foraging alone. The complex maneuvers to successfully hunt prey involve reconnaissance at the surface, exploration, then the actual deep, foraging dive to nab a fleeing salmon, using echolocation to "see" in the dark depths. The noise of nearby vessels makes conditions similar to being at a noisy party and having to keep raising your voice; it's exhausting.

O is for orca. The first half of the killer whale's scientific name—*Orcinus orca*—comes from the Latin for "of the realms of the dead." They're commonly known as killer whales and live in every ocean of the world. The orca the largest member of the dolphin, or toothed whale, family. They have ten to thirteen conical teeth in each jaw that interlock to crush and shred their prey. Orcas swim about seventy-five miles per day. They travel eight miles per hour on average; however, they can burst through the water at thirty miles per hour. Each black and white orca has a unique gray, saddle-shaped patch on the back, enabling researchers to identify them individually.

Orcas, with a capital O. is for an island in the Salish Sea. It's NOT named for orca whales. Rather, it's a shortened form of the name "Horcasitas," part of the full name of Juan Vicente de Güemes Padilla Horcasitas y Aguayo, the Viceroy of Mexico. Horcasitas sent an expedition led by Spanish explorer Francisco de Eliza to the Pacific Northwest in 1791.

P is for pod. Killer whales are highly social, and most live in pods—social groups of a few to twenty or more related individuals seen together more than half the time. The pods have intensely strong family bonds, staying together through the generations for life. They share food, sleep together, play, hunt, explore and travel as a group. Larger groups sometimes form for temporary social interactions, mating, or seasonal concentrations of prey.

Q is for questions. We still have many questions about how to restore the Southern Resident orca population so they're no longer endangered. The most important question: "How can I help?"

R is for resident. In the Pacific Northwest, the group of killer whales that feed exclusively on salmon, ideally Chinook/king salmon, are referred to as residents. They're not to be confused with the first writer-in-residence with the Washington State ferry system (Iris Graville), even though she also eats salmon (but not Chinook). Transient whales feed only on marine mammals. See **S is for Southern Resident Killer Whales** and **T is for transients**.

S is for Southern Resident Killer Whales. In the early 1970s, two separate and distinct populations of fish-eating resident killer whales were found in the Pacific Northwest. These two communities were named in direct relation to their travel patterns in and around the waters of Canada's Vancouver Island. The Southern community of orcas was most often encountered off the southern end of Vancouver Island, including the inland marine waters (the Salish Sea) of Washington State. The Northern community centered in the northern Vancouver Island region, including Queen Charlotte Sound and southern Southeast Alaska. The annual spring-through-summer feeding grounds for the Southern Resident killer whales encompass the inland marine waters of Washington State and Canada. In winter, they follow food along the outer coast, from as far north as Haida Gwaii in British Columbia to as far south as California's Monterrey Bay.

T is for transients. Also called Bigg's killer whales (named after Mike Bigg, known as the father of killer whale research), transients eat other marine mammals, such as seals, sea lions, porpoises and minke whales. This requires different hunting techniques, and thus, a different language. There's no evidence that transients and residents can communicate with each other.

T is also for Tokitae (Sk'aliCh'elh-tenaut). In 1970, Tokitae (also known as Toki and Lolita) was taken from her family in the Salish Sea and, along with some 270 orcas, was placed in captivity. She died at the Miami Seaquarium August 18, 2023. Ocean Sun (L25), is believed to be Tokitae's mother. For years, the Lhaq'temish (Lummi) peoples led campaigns to free the orca known by her Lummi name, Sk'aliCh'elh-tenaut. Southern Residents are central to Lummi language and culture, and they viewed Sk'aliCh'elh-tenaut as "one of them," and a Lummi leader.

Just five months before the whale's death, new owners of the Seaquarium had entered into an agreement with the nonprofit, Friends of Toki, to return her to an ocean sanctuary in the Salish Sea. Residents of J, K, and L pods were all present around San Juan Island the night before she died.

U is for underwater. Killer whales rely on underwater sound to feed, communicate, and navigate. Noise from ocean vessels can interfere with the sounds whales rely on.

V is for vision. The orca's eyes are located on each side of the head, so they don't have binocular vision. Broadly speaking, whales see details about ten times worse than humans and several times worse than your dog or cat. Whales see the world in monochrome, only in shades of gray. The water we see as blue, they see as black. The lens has to do everything in the whale eye; it's circular, instead of flattish like lenses of humans, in order to provide sufficient focus. While humans tread water, whales spy-hop. With their pectoral fins, they position themselves vertically above the water-line, then poke their heads out of the water in a slow, controlled manner. They sometimes stay in this position for minutes at a time to see what's happening at the surface.

W is for Whale Wise. Boat owners approaching too quickly, getting too close, or making too much noise can disrupt orcas, keeping them from finding food, socializing, resting, and other activities. The "Be Whale Wise" campaign, a partnership of governmental agencies, non-profits, and other stakeholders in the Salish Sea, started in the late 1990s to help protect orcas from these disturbances.

After researching best vessel practices to protect the unique and fragile marine resources in the area, the "Be Whale Wise" team helps create consistent messaging and education to commercial and private boaters. U.S. regulations require vessels to stay at least 300 yards away on either side of a Southern Resident Killer Whale's path and 400 yards out of the path in front and behind the orcas.

W is also for weight. Orca calves weigh around four hundred pounds at birth. When they're mature, they can weigh up to six tons.

X is for OnyX. (L87), a male born in 1992. When Onyx's mother died in 2005, he traveled with K Pod until 2010. Then, he began to travel with J8 (Speiden) and J2 (Granny). Even though both Speiden and Granny have died, Onyx remains with J Pod.

Y is for Yoda (K36), a female born in 1993.

Z is for zzzzz—sleeping. Marine biologists believe orcas sleep by shutting down one hemisphere of the brain at a time (see **B is for breathing**), allowing them to rest while still maintaining their voluntary breathing.). They keep the eye on the "asleep" side of the brain open.

In 2018, Iris Graville served as the first Writer-in-Residence for the Washington State Ferries. An earlier version of this essay appears in her latest book, Writer in a Life Vest: Essays from the Salish Sea *(Homebound Publications, 2022), which resulted from that residency. For more information visit irisgraville.com.*

WHY BOTHER?

THE ENVIRONMENTAL COLUMN BY EDITOR, GAIL COLLINS-RANADIVE

Stepping through the front door of the Sun City duplex, I knew in my bones that this was my forever home. After a decade of yearly moves for my ministry career, I was ready to settle down in one place, and this was it!

Once inside, I was captivated by the sweeping views of three of the four mountain ranges that embrace Las Vegas. Moving from the north to the east facing windows, I told the realtor, "Make it happen!"

At that point, I didn't know or even care if it had a kitchen. (It does.)

Nor did I know I'd be able to watch the sunrise moving north to south and back again across the dining room window, from where I'd also glimpse the New Year's Eve and Fourth of July fireworks exploding over the Vegas Strip.

I did not know I'd get to see the moon traverse the southern night sky through the windows above the living room area I'd turn into my study library.

I didn't know I'd be surprised by snow on the mountains visible from my desk in the breakfast nook, or that I'd soon retire from sermon writing and return to writing non-fiction books.

And I didn't know that that sweet space was emitting close to eight metric tons of carbon dioxide into the atmosphere every year.

To get a sense of that magnitude, imagine one metric ton of greenhouse gasses filling a black plastic garbage bag the size of a two-story house. Then multiply that by eight and picture setting these bags out on the curb.

WAYFARER

> *"What is the good of having a nice house*
> *if you haven't a decent planet to put it on.*
> —Henry David Thoreau

———

But instead of heading for the landfill, this waste was being dumped into the atmosphere, adding to the greenhouse gasses that are destabilizing the climate, disrupting weather, disturbing ecosystems, and displacing species.

Did Thoreau somehow know what was coming?

With the Industrial Revolution in full swing in his era, he was acutely aware of the factory run-off polluting his favorite waterways. Also in his era, a French mathematician-physicist recognized there must be a balance between incoming and the outgoing energy to maintain a fairly constant temperature on Earth.

Then, at the end of Thoreau's century, a Swedish scientist noticed a relationship between atmospheric carbon dioxide concentrations and temperature, and was the first to claim that fossil fuel combustion may eventually result in global warming. At that time there were around 280 parts per million of carbon dioxide in the atmosphere, already rising from the constant 278 ppm of pre-industrial times.

And in our era, the 15-year-old great, great, great niece of this father of climate science sat down in front of the Swedish parliament and held up a sign that read "School Strike for the Climate." At that point, five years ago, atmospheric carbon dioxide had reached 407 parts per million.

Other school children joined her, first in Stockholm and then around the globe, demanding their governments take climate action and stop subsidizing the fossil fuel industry (currently being subsidized at 13 million dollars a minute). It made perfect sense to students learning about cause and effect: if increasing levels of carbon dioxide cause the earth's temperature to rise, then stop putting more into the atmosphere. Period.

It is scientifically agreed that 350 ppm is the upper limit of atmospheric carbon dioxide that will maintain and sustain life as we know it, yet many of the countries most responsible for the dangerous increases have already overshot the limits they pledged at the 2015 Paris Climate Accord. Paralyzed into inaction by propaganda and pressure from the fossil fuel industry, many elected officials continue to debunk, deny, delay, deflect, and defer the problem.

Meanwhile, ordinary people have to commit to stop burning fossil fuels for electricity, heating, cooking, and transportation.

As soon as I moved into my owned home, I started inquiring about solar panels for my roof. Initially stymied by Home Owner Association rules, I eventually learned that new state laws trumped city and local regulations, and found a solar company. The eight panels that the local utility monopoly allowed me to put on my roof cut my annual emissions down to four metric tons, while providing all my electricity needs and powering my partner's electric car.

But that left another four tons! Switching out my gas furnace for an air sourced heat pump (its own special nightmare when it kept failing in frigid temperatures) reduced my greenhouse gas emissions another two-plus metric tons, but maxed-out my existing solar panels. I suddenly found myself buying more energy from the utility company that now burns natural gas, a worse greenhouse gas pollutant than was produced by the coal fired power plant we concerned citizens and tribal members had forced them to close.

I clearly needed more solar, especially when I changed out my gas stove for an induction range. While I don't cook much, my partner does, and I worry about the danger of an open flame around aging seniors...not to mention the toxins being spewed into the kitchen from natural gas piped in from elsewhere.

Still, to prepare the kitchen for the induction stove, the electrician had to pull wires from the panel outside the garage and through the attic of the entire house, which cost more than the stove itself.

Why bother!? I was now putting barely one ton into the atmosphere annually! Yet I couldn't ignore that I was still emitting climate-changing greenhouse gasses that, once in the atmosphere, stayed there: as yet there is no human invented way to remove them.

Globally, we've now topped 416 ppm.

So I sought out a new solar company; my previous one had gone out of business with most of the companies in Vegas after the utility company successfully undermined the solar boom it couldn't profit as much from.

If the first solar install was logistical nuisance, the second one quickly turned into a full-blown nightmare. Everything that could go wrong did, even before the contract was signed. And when the install did happen, actually putting the panels on the roof was the one simple part of the whole process.

The accompanying electrical work both outside the house and inside the garage took the electrician 12 hours.

Next, the company contracted to pigeon-proof the panels with heavy screening showed up without the right sizes of mesh and had to order it, which took over a week.

Then the city inspector failed the install. Remedial efforts further delayed the date the panels would be operational.

But then the utility company claimed I wasn't approved for the eight new panels and when the solar company finally got that straightened out, they sent the utility company's inspector to the wrong address, further delaying things.

The project that began in March dragged on through April and into May, when I received a letter of violation from my secondary HOA and learned the solar company had failed to pull the required permits from my community associations. Preparing to present my case for more solar to my neighbor members on the HOA board, what could I say when for most seniors, a Return on Investment was measured in years not decades. It made far more sense to upgrade the kitchen (who doesn't want marble counter tops and sparkling new cabinets?) or remodel

the bathrooms (wouldn't it be wonderful to have new shower doors that didn't require body-wrestling them open when they routinely jumped their warped tracks?), plus the wall to wall carpet *was* wearing out...

And why on earth would I assume full responsibility for my roof and still pay the non-negotiable HOA fees to maintain it as community property? No wonder my home was the only one with solar panels of the forty-eight units in the HOA.

Yet how could I write another environmental column if I didn't walk my talk? How could I look my grandchildren in the face of their deteriorating world if I didn't do what I could to stop catastrophic climate change?

And what would I answer to Gaia, the source and ground of my Being?

When I left Vegas for Denver at the end of May, the solar system was still not operating. A neighbor/friend agreed to open the garage when the time came to flip the switch on, which turned out to be well into June...just ahead of the extreme heat dome that stalled over the entire desert southwest.

I'd like to think that my 16 solar panels pushing energy onto the grid rather than pulling it out helped keep the grid from crashing, and my neighbors from needing to shelter in community cooling centers.

And the last time I checked the readouts from my two sets of solar panels, thus far I have NOT released nearly 30 metric tons of carbon dioxide into the atmosphere, and have produced over 37,000 kilowatt hours of clean electricity...with more to come.

Why bother, indeed.

GAIL COLLINS-RANADIVE SHE/HER is the author of nine published books including *Chewing Sand, Nature's Calling, A Fistful of Stars, Dinosaur Dreaming, Inner Canyon, Where Deep Time Meets Sacred Space* and *Light Year: A Seasonal Guide for Eco-Spiritual Growth*. She also sponsors Homebound's Prism Prize for Climate Literature.

SNAPSHOTS FROM A COLONIZED PLANET

BY SENIOR EDITOR, THEODORE RICHARDS
WITH PHOTOS BY THE AUTHOR

I once taught adult literacy in rural Zimbabwe. One woman came to every class who was so old she didn't know her age or birth date, so old she'd raised children and grandchildren and great grandchildren on what she could grow in the parched earth, the land that the British gave her grandmothers when they'd stolen the fertile land. She'd never held a pencil. I don't recall her name, but I know it began with a C, because that was as far as she ever got: every day, she sat on the ground, practicing her crooked Cs, wrinkled like her skin, while I contemplated the absurdity of having flown halfway around the planet, a 25 year old with liberal arts degree, to teach this woman, who must have had more wisdom in her crooked Cs than in my alphabet of credentials.

I once volunteered at the Missionaries of Charity in Calcutta, where street children with disabilities of various kinds were housed and taught. They came with missing and disfigured limbs, broken bodies and minds. Lice was rampant, so my job was to hold the confused and terrified children down while the nuns shaved their heads. One day, Fergy, the Duchess of York, arrived for a visit. I watched the nuns line up now, like the children lining up to have their heads shaved (but giddy with excitement rather than scared), as she smiled and posed for photos with the bald and broken children.

I once visited a temple in Tibet where children stood outside, playing homemade instruments for pilgrims and tourists. They knew only one word in English: please. There is nothing unusual about this. It could be in Johannesburg or Naples or Rio: The language of commerce and begging is the same worldwide.

THEODORE RICHARDS HE/HIM is a writer, philosopher, educator, and the founder of The Chicago Wisdom Project. The author of eight books, he has received numerous literary awards, including three Independent Publisher Awards and two Nautilus Book Awards. *Reimagining the Classroom*, his latest books, is available wherever books are sold. He lives on the south side of Chicago with his wife and three daughters. You can find out more about him and his work at www.theodorerichards.com.

FINDING MY TRIBE

CANNABIS AS A PATHWAY
FOR HEALING & COMMUNITY
BY ARIANNE RICHARDS

Roots

As a little girl growing up on the south side of Chicago, I would have never thought the adults around me were smoking something that was labeled bad, let alone illegal. I just thought that a joint was "those funny smelling cigarettes," no different than alcohol, and I just knew it was for the grown folks. I spent my early years on 47th and King Drive, the low end, Bronzeville. Bronzeville is where my roots lay in Chicago. I'm a true south side girl through and through.

When I lived in Bronzeville it wasn't the neighborhood that it's becoming now. Those funny-smelling cigarettes weren't the ONLY thing in the air. In those days, Bronzeville reeked of poverty. Some of the things I walked past on a daily basis my kids could never imagine. Bronzeville, just like most of the south side, is categorized as a disproportionately impacted area from the War on Drugs. Even though there was poverty I have some good memories from there as well as some lifelong friends.

While my family moved away from Bronzeville and into the middle class south side neighborhood of Beverly, I never completely left it behind—and also found new struggles as one of the few black kids in the neighborhood. The summer before I started my freshman year of high school was when I first partook in smoking. I wasn't even sure if I smoked the joint right. I didn't think I was high until I got on the bus with my best friend, who is actually more like my sister. We lived around the corner from each other and spent a lot of time at each other's houses and we went everywhere together. So it's really easy to say we smoked a lot of weed together. At the time, I didn't completely know that cannabis was both a way for us to escape from some of our trauma and, at the same time, a way for America to criminalize Black people. One of the traumas we faced was how our communities were being devastated by the war on drugs.

Stunts, Blunts, & Hip Hop

I am a B Girl for life. Hip Hop culture runs deep in my veins. If it wasn't for the culture, I'm not quite sure where I would be now. As I watched some of my friends head off to college, I stayed in Chicago—something I regret at times, but again I wouldn't be who I am today. Hip Hop is how I got involved in community organizing and activism, which has continued to play a major part in my life.

I was (still am, in fact) in a crew called Euphonics/Euphoria. Nancy, the mother of one of the founders of the crew, became a mother of sorts to all of us. Nancy was a huge lover and supporter of the arts. She would allow us to use her basement for our crew meetings every Friday, which would always turn into a creative session full of

freestyling over beats made by crew Djs, breaking, and some would hit the streets to go bombing (graffiti).

During this time, Nancy recognized that I was having a hard time figuring out what to do with myself for work, so she introduced me to Americorps Vista in 1995. This was when I found my early calling of working with youth. I became the assistant youth organizer at Chicago Alliance for Neighborhood Safety.

Friday nights were filled with lots of blunt smoking. It almost felt like a requirement of loving Hip Hop. I'm exaggerating, of course, but it was what we did, very similar to the hippie subculture of the 60's and Jazz before that. Those music genres often spoke about cannabis use that helped spark the creativity of the sound. That promotion of smoking weed also correlates with the fact that these subcultures were looked down upon in mainstream America, but have produced some of the best American music.

The War on Drugs

I had always been a consumer of cannabis, but never had to sell it until I hit a rough patch. In 2000, I moved to Asheville, NC to help my grandmother out with my grandfather who had suffered from heart problems and a couple of strokes. I had only planned on staying there about six months, but that turned into almost three years. I moved out of my grandmother's house and into a really cute 3 bedroom house with two of my friends who were sisters from Michigan. I think we instantly meshed because we were all from the Midwest, the South was definitely a foreign land to us.

I was working at a group home for autistic children and I had a friend named Rose. At the time I was about 23/24 and Rose must've been in her late 50's. Rose was cool as hell and she liked to smoke weed. One weekend she invited me to drive out to see where she lived. She lived on what she called "the way back." It was definitely fucking way back. Mapquest wasn't gonna get me there. This was the type of ride where you are going off the grid. One part of her handwritten directions said to "make a left turn when you get to the old apple tree that is growing through a birdhouse." So of course I took my

roommate with me 'cause I wasn't getting lost in the "way Back" of Appalachia by my Black self. Rose's directions were actually spot on and the drive was worth it. It was definitely a part of the mountains I hadn't experienced yet. Rose was living on a commune of old hippies who were living off of the land. They even had their water coming off the mountain filtered to drink. That was some cold fresh ass water.

Rose introduced us to her friend Robert–also an older guy–who was into Chinese medicine and other holistic practices. I had got Robert's contact and I started buying weed from him. He started coming by the house and hanging out with me and my roommates. He wasn't a stranger around town; Asheville was still a pretty small and intimate place then. One day Robert asked if we wanted to grow in our basement, which felt like a no-brainer since we were spending money on it anyway. We started our adventure, which eventually got

cut short due to spider mites. During this period, Robert and one of my roommates got involved intimately. It became an awkward situation quickly. Robert became manipulating and managed to turn her against me and her sister. He was a master manipulator and a narcissist (which would land him in prison years later). Robert had lost his license to practice medicine 20 years before that because he was growing cannabis and prescribing it to his patients. I obviously don't have an issue with that, but I use this as an example of how he always felt he could do whatever he wanted at whatever cost. What landed him in prison years after I had left Asheville was he was giving cannabis to his young son without his mother's consent or a prescription. When his home was raided they found cannabis plants as well as poppy plants. North Carolina isn't a legal state, medicinal or recreational, but it would be the poppies that got him most of his prison time. I always thought it was bizarre that he would involve himself with opioids, considering it's a major drug crisis.

For me, selling and even buying cannabis always carried a risk. Because it was illegal, there was a violence associated with its sale. And of course there was always a risk that I could get arrested–

plenty of my friends did. But I realized that the law wasn't applied equally. Black people didn't consume, or even sell, cannabis more than white people. We just got arrested in greater numbers. Robert, this older white guy, did whatever he wanted with impunity.

But things were starting to change. I moved to Oakland, California from New York in 2005 shortly after a surgery to remove two ovarian cysts. There, I became a medical cannabis patient. People were starting to recognize that cannabis had many health benefits. But still, my people were going to jail for it.

Finding my Tribe

Back in Chicago, it took a little longer for legalization to arrive, but when it did, I made a decision to shift careers and to work in cannabis. I wanted to work both to educate people about the benefits of cannabis and also try to change laws so my people wouldn't continue to suffer disproportionately from the war on drugs. That's how I got involved with Chicago NORML (National Organization for the Reform of Marijuana Laws).

When I started to get involved with the cannabis industry, I found some of the same inequities, but in a different form. Just as people like Robert used to worry less about being imprisoned for cannabis, I now watched as the legal industry came to be dominated by white men.

In addition to the broader, national mission of NORML to educate the public to destigmatize cannabis and change laws, the Chicago chapter specifically works with communities of color. Through Chicago NORML, I found a group of mostly black and brown women who were working to educate and to change laws about cannabis, and to bring greater wealth through cannabis into marginalized communities that had been harmed by the drug war. But it was more than that. I found my tribe. And to some extent, that was always what cannabis was about. When used responsibly, it has health benefits; when the law is applied equitably, it can bring wealth to disenfranchised communities. But for me, and for the people I know who consume it, it's something to share, a way to build community.

*　　*　　*

A few years ago, I received the terrible news that a close childhood friend had stage 4 colon cancer. She was a fighter, but unfortunately the disease took over her body. We talked about her using cannabis to deal with the side effects from chemo. Whenever she asked, I came through with indica. Even before she went into hospice, I couldn't help but feel helpless. She was going to die, and there was nothing I, or anyone, could do. She had exhausted all the possibilities for a cure, and the medical options were all about making her as comfortable as possible during the time she had left with us. I am forever grateful that this was something that I, and the plant, could help with. Few drugs are as good at relieving the effects of cancer and chemo as cannabis.

So I brought her nature's plant.

But it was more than just relieving physical pain. In sharing cannabis with her, I did what we always did. Just like when I was a young B-Girl in Nancy's basement; like when I first moved to Asheville alone and was looking to find my community; like when I joined Chicago NORML. The plant was a pathway for healing and for taking care of each other, for finding and sustaining community.

———

ARIANNE (ARI) RICHARDS SHE/HER is the Executive Director of Chicago NORML, a nonprofit working to create more equitable and just laws in cannabis in Illinois. She is the founder of Chicago Cannabis Concierge, a personal cannabis consultant and educator, and Certified Professional Interpener (cannabis sommelier). She has a degree in African American Studies and worked as a community activist and educator since the 90s. The former rites of passage and summer camp director at the Chicago Wisdom Project, she currently sits on the board of Wisdom Projects, Inc. Today, she has combined her lifelong love of and commitment to her people with her passion for cannabis to dedicate herself to de-stigmatizing, legalizing, and educating about cannabis in order to give equal access to the emerging industry and to create opportunities for underrepresented communities. Arianne is the mother of three daughters and – after having lived in Asheville, NC, New York City, and Oakland, CA – has returned to live on the south side of Chicago, where she was born and raised.

COLLISIONS OF SCIENCE AND SPIRIT

AN INTERVIEW WITH EMILY GRANDY BY HEIDI BARR

THIS INTERVIEW IS PART OF THE ORDINARY COLLISIONS *INTERVIEW SERIES. LEARN MORE AT HEIDIBARR.SUBSTACK.COM*

The forces in our lives are constantly colliding— sometimes in ways that work out well and sometimes in ways that don't. This interview series is an exploration of what it can look like to work with the collisions, rather than against them. By digging into how humans and nature interact– from our relationships with other humans, to those with our non-human neighbors, to our relationship with ourselves to our relationship with the landbase–we can uncover how to best step fully into our role in the story of the world.

Today's guest on the *Ordinary Collisions Interview Series* is writer Emily Grandy. From what I know about her work and writing, we both value nature connection, social justice/environmental advocacy, exploring diverse landscapes, and have deep roots in the Midwest. Before Emily became a biomedical editor, she did clinical research for a leading academic medical center. Last year, her debut novel, *Michikusa House*, was awarded the Landmark Prize by Homebound Publications. Her forthcoming novel, *Cupido Cupido*, was recently a finalist for the PEN/Bellwether Prize for socially engaged fiction. Her writing has appeared in both academic and literary journals and has been nominated for a Pushcart Prize. She has lived in many places, but always gravitates back to the Midwest and its Great Lakes. She currently calls Milwaukee, Wisconsin home.

Heidi: Emily, Thanks for being here with us today. To start, I always ask the same question: What are two forces that are colliding in your life right now (or that have in the not too distant past)?

Emily: For roughly the last decade, the collision of science and spirit has been on my mind. For me, in my life and my career, these two forces have worked like two opposing magnets that refuse to meet or cooperate. In fact, virtually all my writing explores the reasons why science and spirit are divided. In following the theme of this interview series, today I want to talk about how and why I've endeavored to unite these two forces.

Before I go any further, I guess I should define "science" and "spirit". In this context, I'm referring to the business of science, the methods by which it's carried out, and how the results inform our choices. Specifically, I want to address medicine and biology, as my entire career has been dedicated to those fields (and therefore my critiques do not entirely apply to other disciplines, like physics). Later, as a patient, I also got to see how science translates to clinical practice...and how much can be lost in translation.

I'm using the word "spirit", I admit, partly for the alliteration. But what I'm referring to is wholeness, connectedness, or oneness. The whole essence of a living being, not simply the biology. Even "nature" might be an appropriate stand-in here. As John Muir famously wrote, "When one tugs on a single thing in nature, he finds it attached to the rest of the world." Nature = Oneness.

Okay, moving on. So, let's talk about why I see science and spirit as being divided.

A couple years ago, when I was still working in a lab, I began to feel disenchanted by the world of academia. Like any institution, science has its issues: its methods are imperfect, statistics can be manipulated, funding programs favor hot topics, and funding for medical research is typically only made available to projects with a tangible treatment or product that can eventually be billed to a patient's insurance company. Aside from all that, the white male perspective and Western cultural bias predominate. My own experience within that institution revealed a further shortcoming: the reductive research program.

> "Ancient healing practices like *Ayurveda*, for instance, take a more holistic approach toward health and wellbeing. In Eastern and Indigenous medicine, the aim is not necessarily to treat the symptoms, but to discover why the symptoms arose in the first place . . . the aim is not to find 'a cure' but to achieve balance across all aspects of one's life." — *EMILY GRANDY*

In my novel, *Michikusa House*, the characters grapple with this issue directly. One, an engineer, is said to "[see] the world as an engineering project, an object you can disassemble into its constituent parts which, once identified, can be fully understood. But reductionism only works for objects that can be cleanly separated; it's an impractical method to apply to living, flowing, messy biology."

The best example I can give to illustrate how much medical and biological science overlooks is this: think of the person (other than yourself) who you know best in the world. A spouse or your best friend.

Now imagine your loved one is enrolled in a scientific study in which the researchers' aim is to understand everything about that individual. Every day, for a full year, let's say, scientists from many disciplines will take notes and measurements: blood pressure, cholesterol, hand preference, psychological questionnaires, dream diaries, food intake and exercise, a biographical sketch, genetic profiling, you name it.

At the end, all the scientists pool their data and write a report describing all the metrics they collected and analyzed about your loved one (note that specialists across disciplines rarely collaborate in this way, preferring to work rather a lot in "isolation" within their respective niches). Their combined conclusion is that they now have a pretty good idea of who that person is. But would you say that even after a year of interaction that the scientists know your loved one better than you do? Probably not. Would you even be a little insulted if they claimed to know your loved one better than you do? Probably! Why? Because you are the one who has a relationship with that person. You've known them longer, you have a history together.

My point is this: scientific knowledge, via numbers, rates, and metrics, though undeniably useful and essential to human flourishing, forms an incomplete picture. It is just one way to know something. Forming a relationship is another way—a way to understand the Spirit, a way to know a person in their entirety. Developing relationships is what enriches our lives and gives deeper meaning to our daily interactions.

Indigenous or generational knowledge is also increasingly recognized for its essential wisdom. These ways of knowing can introduce us to the Spirit of every species, body of water, or stretch of land. After all, it's not just people who are complex. Every living thing exists within an intricate ecosystem that is just as nuanced as the life and spirit of your loved one. This sort of knowing, built over long periods, is what facilitates understanding, compassion, and respect for other beings.

Heidi: I could down some many tangents about how metrics miss so many things…… Such an important thing to remember, and dominant culture doesn't often support looking for nuance and prioritizing relationships. How are you navigating the conditions this collision is creating? How does the dissonance created impact your choices?

Emily: In my own writing, I want to share science-based knowledge through storytelling, but also instill a deeper level of respect for other ways of knowing, ways that connect us to the spirit—to the true nature—of other living beings.

Heidi: You're offering your readers such a gift with that approach. What has this collision taught you about yourself? The world?

Emily: I mentioned earlier that I eventually I ended up as a patient for a chronic medical condition at the same institution where I worked, arguably one of the best medical research centers in the country. As in the lab, the physicians and psychologists I met seemed not only to have their own beliefs and agendas, but also viewed me not as a person but as a collection of symptoms to be diagnosed and treated. On the flip side, I also had doctors completely dismiss my symptoms as "all in my head," an unfortunately common habit known as medical gaslighting. I can't even recall how many specialists I saw, but across the board they ignored my "spirit" in favor of their "science". After many years slogging along in this way, and after spending a small fortune, I finally found relief and validation outside Western medicine.

Ancient healing practices like *Ayurveda*, for instance, take a more holistic approach toward health and wellbeing. In Eastern and Indigenous medicine, the aim is not necessarily to treat the symptoms, but to discover why the symptoms arose in the first place. This involves examining diet and sleep habits, exercise and activity, stress levels, our relationships, even the seasons and the weather can influence a person's flourishing. Because these elements shift from day to day, the aim is not to find "a cure" but to achieve balance across all aspects of one's life. Only after extending care to each element of my entire self—to every part of my spirit—versus treating only the symptoms, did I finally begin to find wellness. It is a much longer process, goodness knows, but the rewards, in my experience, are far superior and significantly longer lasting.

My symptoms never fully vanished, but I learned an important lesson: the resolution of pain is not the end goal of holistic living. Pain is actually an essential component of health. It teaches you listen to your body and respect its needs. Eventually you can learn to notice the minute shifts in your body's energy, your emotions, and then respond accordingly to rebalance the equilibrium before you even approach the pain stage. Practices like yoga, meditation, and massage which work to recalibrate the mind, body, and breath are therefore considered to be not the occasional hobby, accessible only to those who can afford spa treatments and island retreats, but essential components to wellbeing.**Heidi:** Oh my gosh yes. I can relate to this so much from my own experience with a lingering illness. Listening to our bodies, and trusting what they share, is so important.

Heidi: Can you tell us a bit about a collision you explore in your book that's due out soon?

Emily: My debut novel, *Michikusa House,* tackles this issue—the collision between science and spirit—head on. In the book, the main character is a young woman recovering from an eating disorder. Although she's healed in body, she hasn't yet found a reason to want to get better. Thanks to a family connection, she ends up spending a year on a small family farm in rural Japan, digging—quite literally—into the rich food culture of that country, learning to grow vegetables and cook in concert with the seasons. In fact, she's learning to cook for the first time in her life. In this way, she begins to reconnect with the living world, while simultaneously shedding long-held beliefs about shame, identity, and renewal. After returning to her hometown in Ohio, she fails to find that same sense of wholeness and connection in her undergraduate nutrition science program. Ultimately, she abandons the goal of obtaining a degree in favor of reconnecting with earth, taking a job as a groundskeeper at the historic cemetery behind her apartment.

Although it is entirely a work of fiction, *Michikusa House* draws on my own healing experience. It takes a critical view of contemporary nutrition science and American food culture while exploring the transformative power that comes from connection with other living things, humans and non-humans alike.

Heidi: I did my master's thesis on eating disorders and I come from a family of organic vegetable farmers, so I'm really looking forward to reading!

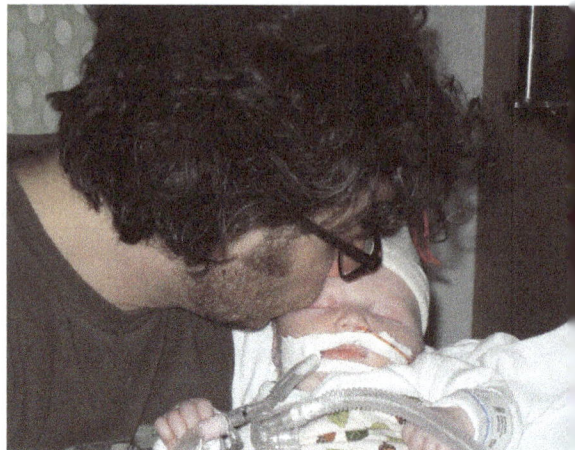

THE MOURNING RUN

Mid-February

Snow melting

Ground is slushy

I don't mind if my socks get wet

I'll continue to run

Leaping over big puddles

And crunching on thin ice

My playlist is on shuffle

As the chatter is on repeat

Thinking of you

It's always about

You

Again

And again

And again

All this breath work

This Mindfulness

Is exhausting

Be in the moment, they say

But *they*, don't know.

Be still, I tell myself

And I try

For tomorrow

Coffee first

And then out for another

mourning run.

THE MOURNING RUN

HOW RUNNING. . . HELPED.

BY ROBERT BRODER

After my daughter Stella was born not breathing, and hours later leaving my wife at the hospital to sit in an ambulance heading to an emergency NICU in Boston, to find out she is brain damaged globally and will have no chance of life, 12 days later she took her last breath in my arms . . . now what?

So that was it, just leave the hospital and go back to everyday life. Like the past nine months never happened. The excitement of welcoming a baby, the singing, hugging, and kissing my wife's belly, the prep into making her room so special... all for no reason.

We're just supposed to go back to work and deal with the regular socialization we all must do in everyday life. Like nothing even happened. Yet, your body, your brain, your soul is frozen. Frozen in time, in thoughts, in dreams, in feelings, in every breathing moment.

MY DAUGHTER JUST DIED!

You don't expect a nurse to ask you what you would like to do with the body of your 12-day old daughter—finding myself two days after she died, pulling into the funeral home parking lot, picking up her ashes in a hypnotic state.

After Stella died, my wife and I, and our dog Alice, got in the car and headed out west. The thought of going back to work and regular life things was not even an option. The Grand Canyon was the main destination. No other reason than we just couldn't stay home. With Stella's room all set for her, she would never get to see a space with the beautiful mural Amanda painted with a tree and an owl and a moon. The crib and cute mobile we bought. The changing table and rocking chair we meticulously picked out. All the things from the baby shower were completely irrelevant. We closed the bedroom door to our two-bedroom home and headed west. When we got to Moab, we hiked around Arches National Park and Canyonlands. And when we were alone, we'd cry. I'd think about why we were there and how we didn't want to be. We thought we should be at home with Stella doing all everyday new baby things. When we made it to the Grand Canyon, Amanda said, "I'm ready to head home. And if you want, I will try again."

When we got home, everything was still in a different reality. What do you mean I have to go back to work? What do you mean I have to go grocery shopping and communicate like a normal person contributing to society. My daughter just died. I want Stella! I want nothing else!!!! My head would scream over and over. I wanted to scream in public, but that would seem insane or irrational. But nothing is normal when you're in this mind-bent state.

Someone said we should try to go to a bereavement group and meet other families who had lost babies and children. So one brave night, we did. I didn't know what to expect. Like I would click with another dad and be like, hey, you lost a baby too, let's be friends. But after the short meet and greet, it immediately was not for us. Everyone sat in a circle sharing their stories, what happened to their babies, and the stories people were sharing were so unbelievably sad. It made how we were feeling even more difficult to bear. We heard countless stories about child suicide, car accidents, or cancer. For us, it was malpractice. The nurse and doctor read the monitors wrong and didn't see Stella was under stress for over three hours during labor. And, all of our children were gone.

Amanda and I also started seeing therapists. Either together or alone. It seemed to be the only option to get us through this healing process. Since we never found another couple or person that experienced what we went through. We didn't talk to family or friends because it's such an unbelievably sad topic that no one seemed to want to hear about it or talk about it. We would cry to each other until we fell asleep. And I would wake up and quietly say to myself, "Fuck, I'm still here."

And then, only two months after Stella died, Amanda got pregnant. Our reaction was very somber. Ok, let's see what happens. It took us a while to get pregnant with Stella, so we assumed it would take just as long again. It felt very déjà vu. Pregnant again. I still don't know how Amanda did it, and later she said it felt like being pregnant for two years straight.

After Eleanor Moon was born (Moon from Stella's mural) from a thankfully wonderful normal birth (complete opposite from Stella), the heaviness of depression, anger, and sadness became stronger and more powerful inside of me.

Now what? I couldn't handle a screaming baby and care for her while I was still mourning Stella and what went so tragically wrong. There were days, weeks, months where Amanda did everything to care for Eleanor while I just sat on the couch, either watching tv or staring out the window doing nothing. Taking care of Eleanor and being in the moment was something I couldn't do, for in my mind, I was clearly holding Stella and her last breath in my arms.

I was not bonding with Eleanor. The more she cried and screamed, the more I wanted to be somewhere else. And all I wanted was for Stella to be here. I had zero desire to do any normal dad or parenting stuff.

Even though Eleanor got to see the room we made for Stella, we still felt like there was darkness in the house or maybe with us. So we sold our two-bedroom home and moved into a nice place on two acres of land in rural Massachusetts. I believed the move would help us heal and get some type of normalcy back. It did not.

Being out in the beautiful woods with no friends or nearby family with nothing to do in zero-degree weather with a newborn made things worse. Solitude was not the answer. I was also a sales rep. So being alone in the car for eight hours a day and putting on a pretend face when visiting customers is no medicine for depression or healing from the loss of your baby.

I wanted to leave. I never wanted to wake up again, and I wanted to get myself out of this painful mental pressure. So we sold that house at a loss, and there seemed to be no answer except to quit my good-paying job and move to Portland, Oregon. The farthest possible spot from where Stella was born, so we would never have to drive past that hospital again. And we chose the opposite of rural—a crowded, vibrant city.

Even though Portland is fun and funky, it did not solve the problem either. Years later, after Stella died and all the moving transitions, I still had no desire to do anything, and I still wasn't bonding with Eleanor, who was turning five years old.

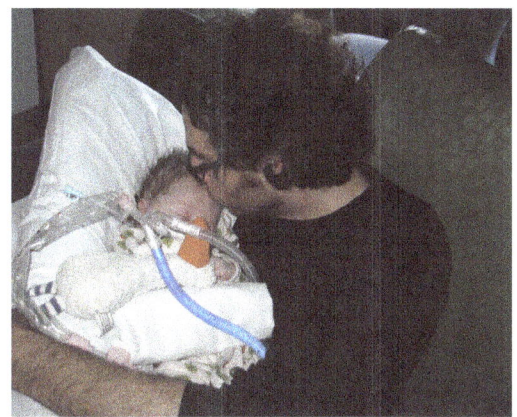

We took our savings and started a children's picture book publishing company, which consumed my thoughts. I wanted something to succeed. I talked and thought about it every day. So much so that one night at dinner, Amanda said, "Can we please talk about something else."

I just wanted every book we made to be so good. I wanted the books to be beautiful and well-received, and this became my creative outlet. I was designing books and learning about the publishing world. But Amanda wasn't happy, and I wasn't focusing my time on Eleanor or my family. I focused on trying to be happier. Every day I walked through the streets of Portland. And Amanda found a way to be supportive and patient with me, just trying not to be so depressed. She made positive suggestions like meditation, yoga, or even a pottery class—anything to get my smile back.

Since she never knew what kind of mood I'd be in at any given moment, sad, mad, quiet, or completely dark, she took a risk. More therapists just kept telling me to cry it out and journal my thoughts. Or concentrate on my breathing.

We lived in Portland for four years, and neither of us could find a job, and publishing books wasn't making us money, so Amanda said, "I applied for a job at UVM. If I get the job, I think we should move back home." Vermont is where we first met, but I also lived there two other separate times in my life. It always seems to call me back.

Since I had no desire to wake up each morning, moving to Vermont was the last place I wanted to go. But Amanda, being so sweet, got the job through a video interview, and one month later, we packed up everything we owned and headed back east into a rental outside of Burlington. We pulled Eleanor out of first grade, only to start her in a new first grade class two weeks later.

I remember her crying while driving through Wyoming, "I want to go home. I want to go home!" She meant Portland. We both hugged her, as I soothed her with the most comforting words I knew. "Where ever we are, is home," I said. What I was doing to myself was also affecting her and my family. I wanted to remove these dark clouds, the cinderblock on my chest, the painstakingly painful thoughts, but I didn't know how. I didn't want to live the rest of my life feeling so much pain.

Now what? Eleanor started school, and Amanda began her new job, which left me (besides working on the press) to do absolutely nothing. I did not want to be here. After all, it would be my third time moving back to the green mountain state. I even told Amanda as much one day in a rude text while she was at work. And I was so depressed and angry and sad that I couldn't even stand being alone with myself. I couldn't find a job, nor did I want a job. I felt unqualified and unconfident to do anything. I didn't care how much money we had left. And again, more therapists with the same bit of advice. After telling him my entire backstory, one of the last therapists I saw asked, "Do you ever have a good cry?"

On my 49TH birthday, Amanda and Eleanor went away for the weekend. And I said to myself, when I turn 50, I'll go skydiving. Because it was the one thing I was afraid to do. At that exact moment, I called the closest place around and signed up. And all I could think of was, if the chute doesn't open, I don't have to think of all the sadness and feel this pain anymore.

But one day, while walking through some nearby woods, which I did any chance I could because it was the only thing that somewhat calmed my chattering mind, my walk turned into a jog. And my jog turned into a run. I might have run 75 yards that day before stopping, out of breath. The next day, I did the same thing, walk - run - walk. And while talking to myself with all the negative and maddening thoughts in my head, the running became longer. Until one day, only a few weeks later, I ran a full mile without stopping, the entire length of the path.

I didn't tell Amanda I started running because I didn't want to mention it, only to stop running a few weeks later, and it was only a short phase. But she noted that I seemed more "even." I didn't know what to say. Maybe I was a bit calmer. I hadn't changed anything in my life, except that I started running. So I told her and wondered aloud if that had anything to do with it. And the look from Amanda said, well, whatever it is you're doing, keep doing it. I kept running.

I bought a cheap pair of running sneakers, because I thought, don't make a big investment if you stop like everything else you've tried. My one mile became two miles. My dirt path changed with the seasons to mud and snow and ice. And I'd get dressed in thermals and sweatpants. And, I ran.

Even if my fingers and face were freezing from the cold, I'd run even just a little to get out of my screaming head. I would just talk to myself. I would talk to my mom, who passed away when I was a freshman in high school, and I would speak to Stella (named after my mom). Wishing she was here and I could hold her.

When the conditions outside became too challenging to run, I joined a 24-hour fitness place, only to use the treadmill. And since I slept so poorly, I'd be there at 4 am, no one else there, and run. I would run until I felt like stopping or for one more good song that came on my iPod. I even signed up for my first 5k, and when I finished, I was surprised how short it was.

One day while running my usual farm trail, I did it twice and ran over seven miles. I was so surprised and happy with myself that I patted myself on the back. Which then pushed me to run my first half-marathon.

Running became an everyday routine for me. Coffee, run, breakfast. As I would fall asleep at night, I was already looking forward to the next morning's run. When I got there so early, I would sometimes see coyotes heading home after their mischievous night. It was like some type of endorphins were jolting inside of me. If I missed a day, I would feel disappointed. It became my meditation, my therapy, my temple. Some days I'd run 20 minutes, others I'd run 45 minutes.

I would run and say, I don't want to be here! If there is a god, please take me! Strike me, please, and end everything right now! I'm so tired of hurting. I'm so tired of living! Anything to get rid of this awful pain!

I started to notice I was more me. I was silly with Eleanor, wrestling with her, trying to make her laugh, and leaving sweet notes for Amanda just to try and make her smile.

But one day, while I was running, I was talking to Stella. Telling her how much I missed her and how sorry I was that everything went so horribly wrong, and then I felt her hug me. A huge wave of emotion came over me like a bolt of lightning struck through my chest, and a tear ran down my face.

As the months passed by, I would say, Where's my joy? I want to feel joy. Bring me joy.

I became more present in my time with Eleanor and Amanda, and I wasn't so distant in my thoughts. The depression, the anger, the sadness lifted a bit. I became more mindful, less depressed, angry, and sad. I eventually bought better running sneakers and thermals, and now I just go outside and run any chance I get. In a way, I wish one of the therapists would have suggested I try running. Maybe I would have listened.

With the support and patience from my wife, the love and sweetness from my daughter, and the beautiful Vermont country trails, finding my way to run helped me heal, and become more still and silent in my everyday living. Which is where I like to be.

ROBERT BRODER HE/HIM is a children's book author and founding publisher of award-winning Ripple Grove Press. He is the writer of Patagonia's first picture book titled *Better Than New*. Other books include *Crow & Snow* (Simon and Schuster) and *Our Shed* (Little Bigfoot) which received a Kirkus Starred Review. He enjoys walking in the snow, running at the farm, hiking in the woods, and drinking coffee on the couch. He lives with his family in a small town, near a big lake, surrounded by green mountains. He is Poet Laureate of Shelburne, Vermont. See more at RobertBroder.com

WHEN YOU GET TO BE OLD
BY GUNILLA NORRIS

I am not done with my changes.
— Stanley Kunitz

When you get to be old
losses are the way of things.
They are like scattered treasures
abandoned on the long trek
out West while seeking your fortune.

The family silver, too heavy for the wagon,
is set by the rise of a steep hill, and the bureau
with your soft feminine dreams and silks
will be left by a stream, drawers open to rain.

You get the weathered boards of the wagon
instead, with the wheels under it rumbling
along for years, tipping this way and that.
You get nights full of stars and strangeness.

You get the far country where you won't
know anyone and where many things live
that you'll never care to know. Why not
make camp in the living room? Why not

arrive where you already are? It is as good
a place as any to find what remains …
a small stack of kindling, flint, split wood,
the smell of smoke and the moist steam

from your kettle with its humble dings
shining in the moonlight and on you, too,
as you crawl out of the worn wagon
to make camp and be here as it is.

DESERT INDIGO
by Gunilla Norris

In here it's quiet … so very quiet,
yet, through the window
I can hear the whizz of cars
and the wailing of the ambulance

on the way to a possible rescue.
Am I in need of rescue in the shared
pandemic fear that enwraps me
like the nap of a fathomless velvet,

thick and dark, the color of desert indigo?
It is so quiet … I easily hear my neighbors
laughing on the common stairs to my living
room along with the clank of a garbage truck.

It is so quiet that the world just walks
right in and sits on the sofa, shattered,
tearful and without taking a single visible breath
keeps talking. I listen. There's nothing better to do.

We're so briefly here. Give me your hand.
We have this moment to be broken and rescued,
knowing we are here together teetering
on the edge, enwrapped with one another.

_____

Both selections from Norris' new poetry collection, *Old and Singing.*

THE UNRELIABILITY OF THE HEART
BY EDITOR-AT-LARGE, THOMAS LLOYD QUALLS

Forget everything I've told you about the heart. Forget what all the books and the gurus and the masters have said. The heart cannot be trusted.

Seriously, beware. It is reckless and selfish and has no regard whatsoever for your safety. Or your happiness. It will lead you straight into temptation. Into the fire and over cliffs. Then shrug its shoulders at the wreckage. If you don't believe me, just think about the trouble it has caused in your own life. See? I told you. Why have we unwittingly given the heart so much power over our lives? It feels like we didn't even have a choice. Like we came wired that way from the factory.

Consider this your wake-up call. You do not have to believe everything it says. You do not have blindly follow it down questionable alleyways. You do not have buckle at the knees at its slightest provocation. And you most certainly do not have to rethink everything in your life and change your whole trajectory because it tells you to. I mean, unless that's what you really want. But how do you even know what you really want? How do you even know what you really think?

Not that thinking is any more reliable. Your head should wipe that smug look off its face, because it does not have any better track record. How many times has it thought something was a good idea that clearly was not. And then, in the wake of any bad decision, it starts thinking the only way for you to be in the world is to play everything safe. To avoid feelings at all cost. And so you end up sitting alone with nothing to do. Trying to remember why there is no joy in your life. Who designed these stupid human bodies of ours? Someone should file a products liability lawsuit against the manufacturer. Both the heart and the head would make terrible witnesses at trial, though. They're not reliable narrators. Each one always wanting to blame the other.

If neither the head nor the heart can be trusted to guide us, then what are we supposed to do?

Maybe we should we hold some kind of peace summit and negotiate a treaty between them. Do you think it is possible for them to talk to each other and see if they can work out some kind of an information sharing arrangement? I think it's worth a shot. I mean what do we have to lose? Things aren't exactly working the way they are.

Hopefully the whole is better than the sum of its parts.

THOMAS LLOYD QUALLS HE/HIM is a writer, a condition that is apparently incurable. Thomas is the author of two novels and a collection of essays. He is a former copywriter and music festival owner, a licensed attorney who has overturned two death sentences, and a one-time vagabond who regularly wandered the globe with a backpack and three changes of clothes.

AN EXCERPT FROM

THE MIKE FILE

by Stephen Trimble

I am a person with great determination, power, desire, initiative, and confidence in myself. I am getting by in this big deep revolving world.
-Mike's letters to Isabelle, June 6th and 29th 1967

YOU STEP FROM YOUR CAR, distracted, headed for an appointment. A homeless man approaches. Bearded, unkempt, wild-eyed. You know you should be empathetic, but he comes too close. No sense of boundaries, no filters, jumpy in his movements. You pull back, you stiffen, on alert, expecting a request for a handout or a disorganized rant about lurking CIA operatives.

You feel guilty, but you don't want to get drawn into messiness. You nod, you smile tightly. You look away. You move on.

Mike may have had some of this look of The Other, even if I remember him cleaner, better dressed, and better groomed than most of the people we see walking on downtown sidewalks, conversing in erratic outbursts with unknown listeners. Most of us turn away from these people in need, no matter how forlorn they seem. We don't want to get involved.

Mike never retreated from his painful decision to cut off contact with us. We honored his appeal to be left alone. And he wasn't the only returning patient to lose connections with family. The vast majority of people released from the state hospital did not return home. They had no families to take them in.

The Galvins were an exception. In this tragic and astonishing family—so vividly described in Robert Kolker's 2020 book, *Hidden Valley Road*—ten of the twelve children are boys, and six of these boys are diagnosed with schizophrenia. They live in Colorado Springs. Beginning in 1970, they cycle between the state hospital and their home throughout their lives. "Pueblo" carries the same weight in their family as in ours. But the Galvin brothers lived in a new era of care that rejected warehousing patients for decades. The family was determined to keep them in their circle—a fierceness built from both love and denial.

In Mike's day, nearly everyone leaving the hospital in Pueblo ended up in halfway houses, boarding houses, or, eventually, on the streets. In Colorado, the community-based services needed for effective housing and treatment couldn't cope with the flood of patients migrating out of Pueblo. With time, resources grew ever more scarce.

Coming to Denver "paroled" as an ex-state hospital patient, Mike carried nearly the same stigma he would have endured if he'd been released from prison. The language we use to describe people like Mike matters. We react differently to "retarded and schizophrenic" than we do to "people with intellectual disabilities and psychiatric illness."

When I was a kid, one way to cope with my brother's banishment was to picture Mike living in the best possible situation for someone like him, a sort of boarding school, a place he accepted, adapted to, maybe even preferred. After he left the hospital and cut himself loose from us, I could imagine him as an independent actor, with a circle of similar folks to hang out with. But I never visualized details. I had no starting point.

Meanwhile, I took my peaceful and privileged life with our parents for granted. I acknowledged my brother just once a year. At least through high school, I sent Mike presents for Christmas and for his New Year's Eve birthday. Aftershave. A carton of cigarettes. He sent a brief thank you. And then I returned to my classes, my friends, my enthusiasms, giving him no thought, sometimes for months.

The final diagnosis in Mike's chronology at discharge in spring 1967 brands him with a lifetime label, "Schizophrenic reaction, residual type." The patchy record makes no mention of "retardation." Psychiatric disorder evidently trumped intellectual disability. The very last line marks his official discharge from the hospital in October 1967, a year after his arrival in Denver: "*Condition, Improved—Administrative Discharge.*"

STEVE, WEARING HIS COWBOY DUDS AT 4 1/2, MIKE AT 12; DENVER, 1955.

How "improved" was he? What happened to his "schizophrenia?" Controlled? No reports from Pueblo can tell me. And Denver General Hospital has no files from outpatients who used their services so long ago. The record lists two last Capitol Hill addresses with October dates. And that's it. Mike disappears.

I saw Mike one additional time, walking across a street in downtown Denver as I drove by. Again, I didn't stop. I'm surprised I didn't run into him more often. Denver hadn't hit its big growth spurt in these years. It still felt like a small city, but not small enough for Mike and me to cross paths frequently on my visits home.

LET IT BE

On a cold winter-gray day in 1970, I drive through downtown Denver in our inelegant old pinkish-tan 1962 Dodge Dart, the family car now passed on to me. I'm home from college on winter break, running errands. Multi-lanes of traffic carry me down Broadway, through the heart of the city, the heart of the state. The Capitol rises to my left, its gold dome incandescent in low-angled light. Off to the right, khaki-colored grass leads past leafless black branching trees reaching skyward, the imposing Civic Center behind. Steam plumes from vents. The breath of the city.

A line of people stands on the curb, bundled up for winter, waiting, watching, or maybe just killing time. And there's Mike, at the front of a cluster of folks at a bus stop. He wears that same scowl of unhappiness I remember. He's a slouching column of dark tallness, a cigarette dangling from his fingers.

I slow down, I grip the wheel, hesitant, agitated, but can't quite get myself over to the curb. I want to stop. I'm scared to stop. My AM radio blasts The Beatles—*The Long and Winding Road that leads me to your door...* and *Let It Be.* Conflicting advice. No help there.

I'm riveted to Mike as I roll by. He doesn't make eye contact. Even if he saw me, he might not recognize me. Mike wanted nothing to do with us, right? What in the world would I say?

I don't pull over, roll down the window, call to him.

Before I know it, I'm past, still clutching the wheel. I do not drive around the block to give myself a second chance to push through my uncertainty, stop, park, hop out of the car, and catch Mike before he moves on, boards his bus, disappears. I let the current of traffic carry me downstream, south along Broadway, away from my brother.

My recollection of this encounter *moves*, like a scene from a movie, a YouTube video clip. It's one of those permanent memories generated when you lock onto a scene, staring so hard at someone or something that there's a taut line carrying the image right into your brain where it remains forever vivid.

After so many years of Mike existing as an abstract fact in the nether reaches of reality, without detail or motion, this chance sighting of my brother takes on the full resonance of regret. I remember the moment with utter clarity because I'm so mortified by my failure to call out to him. I simply don't have the confidence, the empathy, the kindness, the agency, to stop.

HEROES IN THE ALMSHOUSE

We had no contact with Mike for nearly ten years. In that decade, I matured, slowly. I celebrated birthdays from 16 to 26. I won a scholarship to college; traveled as far as Europe, Israel, South America; became a mountaineer, a park ranger; began grad school; published my first small pieces of writing, with my photographs. With one weak eye and no depth perception, I escaped the Vietnam-era draft despite my low lottery number. I was on my way to what most would call the normal adulthood of a privileged straight white male.

Mike always maintained his distance, though he accepted small checks from our mother for spending money. He never contacted our parents or me about a visit. Did he sometimes consider a call or waver in his ferocity? The 1967 letters show agonizing ambivalence. Did our parents try to break through his barriers? I know I did not.

Mike still came into my Uncle Harry's downtown Denver jewelry store occasionally. He wrote to Charlotte. He reached out to his aunt and uncle, who hadn't sent him to the state hospital.

Mike admired Char and Harry. They cultivated an aura of affluence. They were embedded in Denver's Jewish business community. They weren't his parents. Mike couldn't have picked up a strong Jewish identity from our adamantly anti-organized-religion mother, but he might have *chosen* to think of himself as Jewish to locate himself in a world closer to his aunt.

Mike's quiet life in Denver could have been a function of his disabilities, his illness, his childhood trauma. External forces didn't help. Paternalistic boarding home operators and the dependable arrival of disability checks encouraged passivity and idleness. And years on numbing neuroleptics have a permanent deadening effect. Psychotropic drugs save lives, but when I read writer and activist Robert Whitaker, he emphasizes the wrenching trade-off: "...people who tolerated neuroleptics well, and weren't 'relapsing,' were living purposeless, isolated, and largely friendless existences."

My father maintained remarkable empathy for his troubled stepson throughout these years. Mike's life sparked my father's evolution from small-town Republican to passionate believer in the Democrats' societal safety-net. Dad had rejected his family's conventional Christianity long ago in grade school. But he didn't move on from the conservative politics he grew up with until he experienced Mike's struggles. As he later explained to anyone who would listen, especially his least progressive friends, we can't all pull ourselves up by our bootstraps. For the rest of his life, Dad told this story as the parable that redefined his political identity.

His tutorial went like this. Mike was born needing help from his community. I was born eight years later, securely holding the world by the tail. Mike came with a history that set him apart, and society was ready to brand him a failure and sideline him as a threat. I came with a stable emotional baseline and workable intelligence. This chasm between possibilities, and the need to compassionately address that gap, turned Dad into a progressive, a social liberal. Through all the tumult of America's next fifty-five years, he only grew more disgusted with our abandonment of those in need. In his nineties, he emphatically described himself as a "radical Democrat."

Mike logged his nine years of confinement at the hospital and emerged with his discharge certificate, "improved." He returned to Denver and lived on his own for another ten years. And yet society has trouble thinking of him as a fellow citizen and community member who happens to have a brain that works differently. No one ever described him as a young man who demonstrated real bravery when he faced each new day.

He must have spent these years in group homes (also called board-and-care homes), "the modern version of the almshouse...a community-based back ward," as writer and therapist Ann Braden Johnson puts it.

Mike wasn't so much deinstitutionalized as reinstitutionalized for his last decade. Federal welfare covered his board and room and a bit of spending money. Cigarettes, a movie. Bowling, perhaps. Medicaid covered his drug expenses and whatever therapy he received.

Minimally licensed, group homes had one primary mission, to make money for the owner. Apart from a brief interlude of well-funded follow-up care, Mike went from warehoused inmate to commodit Neither role gave much thought to his humanity or his needs. President John F. Kennedy's plan fc federally funded community mental health treatment hadn't worked sustainably for Mike and h peers. They remained mostly on their own.

LOVE, WORK, PANCAKES

A widely-quoted aphorism from Freud tells us that "Love and work are the cornerstones of ou humanness." Mike, as far as I know, had few avenues for either.

As I try to conceive of Mike's happiness, how he structured his life to meet his needs as best h could, I think of *Rain Man*. Mike wasn't Raymond Babbitt, the Rain Man so memorably acted b Dustin Hoffman, and I'm not Charlie, the arrogant hotshot younger brother played by Tom Cruise. But Charlie spends a week with his *savant* brother on their memorable road trip and makes "a connection." That experience transforms their relationship. Charlie, self-involved and selfish, for the first time can say of Raymond, the brother he had forgotten, "This is my family."

At the end of the movie Charlie harangues Raymond's doctor. "Did you spend 24 hours a day, seven days a week with him? Have you ever done that? When we started out together, he was only my brother in name. And this morning... we had pancakes. I made a connection."

Mike (13), Stevie (5), and Don (40). Summer, 1956.

It never occurred to me to seek out Mike, for pancakes, for connection, for anything at all. His place in my life was defined by a rote explanation whenever I got around to mentioning him. The best I could muster was to add new phrases to my mantra as Mike added new chapters in his life. *"I have a retarded brother—a half-brother. He left home when I was six when he was swept away by schizophrenia. He spent years at the state hospital and now lives in a halfway house and wants nothing to do with our family."*

His existence barely mattered to me in these years. But his existence always mattered to our mother.

So did his death.

Continue reading *The Mike File,* now available in paperback, ebook and audiobook.

AN AUTUMN EXHALE

(AND APPLE COFFEE CAKE)

THE MINDFUL KITCHEN BY HEIDI BARR

October 6. I've just finished wiping off the jars of applesauce that I canned this morning. Late afternoon sunlight shines through the leaves, creating dancing shadows thanks to a brisk wind. It's not quite the peak of autumn color yet, but some trees are blazing red and orange. I like this time of year, despite feelings of busyness due to yard and garden work, the quest to acquire enough firewood, and winterizing things. Squashes are ripe, and there are still green vegetables to enjoy straight from the earth. It may freeze next week, so it's been a time of roasting, freezing, and baking to preserve the harvest. It's a time of abundance even though time can feel scarce. I inhale and keep working.

October 12. The first snow of autumn is here–just a dusting that's melting as the evening air grows just warm enough. Wind whips my hair around my face when I venture outside for a few minutes, and the fully yellowed maples are quickly losing leaves. Everything is damp and a little droopy, but the freeze hasn't yet come. Peppers and tomatoes are still fruiting, and some have new blossoms, even this late in the season. They're hanging on despite the fact they won't reach maturity. Back inside the internet is down. This is a welcome, if not wanted, respite from too much virtual connection. An empty muffin tin waits on the counter for batter. The sky is flat gray, but tiny water droplets dot fallen leaves on the grass, each one a world in itself, a world of cyclical light, a world of transition and turning.

October 14. Brilliant light bounces off of gold foliage, reminding me that autumnal evening paddling is nothing short of astonishing. I can see my breath as the air cools. The sun dips behind the trees as I paddle back toward the dock. In the shallows I see an enormous snapping turtle just under the surface of the water, near some decomposing lily pads. She swims right under the canoe. Her presence reminds me of all the life that exists outside my window, outside my screens, outside my human-focused agenda. She makes me want to be a better human, a better planetary neighbor, a better ancestor. She is a part of me, and she deserves a chance to thrive in clean waters, undisturbed. She makes me think about climate disruption and colonization and how badly humans still treat one another and the

planet. What is my role in reparations toward the marginalized groups of people who are alive now? How do I best show up in daily life as an anti-racist, as a person who accepts where and when I entered the collective story? What does it mean to be a good ancestor? How do I move in wider circles? How do I live slower in a world that seems to speed up with every passing moment?

There are no clear, easy answers to these questions. Yet it remains important to ask them. And ask them again and again until a way forward is carved from the persistent effort to change the dominant cultural narrative for good. My ancestors came from a land across the sea, land I have never visited. But I live here, now, on land where primarily Dakota and Ojibwe people lived (and, of course, many of their descendants still do) until European settlers colonized it. It's land to which I feel connected, even with its complicated history. I must keep asking the questions and listening to the answers that may well be discerned from very different actions: Paying attention to the pause between gusts of autumn wind. Scouring the community for local stories that tell the true history of the land. Listening to the lived experiences of others, from humans to elderly snapping turtles, existing and persisting all these years as time churns on. Allowing slowness to be an acceptable speed at which to operate.

October 28. I am in the garden, hauling a bale of hay to mulch the garlic that was just planted. I look up at the sound of flapping to see eight sandhill cranes soar west to land in the field across the road. At 38 degrees, the air is cooler than it has been in months. Even though I'm not yet used to the cold temperatures, I'm glad for them. Planting the garlic always seems to signal a downshift from bustling autumn to early winter stillness. Most of the leaves have now fallen. Trees stand bare against a gray sky. Leaves that linger catch attention with flashes of burnt umber and gold in a long line of naked branches. Summer this year went by quickly, and it's hard to believe it's already time to change the routine from hoeing and harvesting to splitting wood and shoveling snow. But change comes, and we adapt.

October 30. The house is quiet, except for the crackle of fire and the soft sounds of a guitar. Flames reach toward the ceiling of the wood stove. Music expands into the empty spaces of the room. The house is cradled in darkness this late in the day. A car goes by outside, its dull hum barely discernible. What seems to matter is that in the foreground, that which is close at hand, within easy earshot or tangible distance. Things far away still matter, but in a different way (not more and not less) than what is happening right here, right now. I wonder if paying attention to what's right in front of me could be one way to cope with the uncertainty of the times, with the uncontrollable. I wonder if I can help make the circle wider by tending to my own roots, so I have the strength to extend my branches fully.

Flames continue to reach, and harmonies fill the empty spaces. The cats stretch out next to the hearth, content to sit still in the glowing warmth of the fire. Another log goes on. Flames lick higher and warmth reaches further. Days shorten. Nights lengthen. Time catches up to abundance, and I exhale into whatever's coming next. I hope I remember to move slow enough to inhale fully the goodness that awaits when I do.

This piece is included in the 2022 anthology released by Homebound Publications called In *Search of Simple.*

HEIDI BARR SHE/HER is a writer and wellness coach whose work is founded on a commitment to cultivating ways of being that are life-giving and sustainable for people, communities, and the planet. She is the author of several books of creative nonfiction, including *Collisions of Earth and Sky* and *Woodland Manitou*, and co author of *12 Tiny things*. She's also authored two poetry collections, one cookbook, and is editor of "The Mindful Kitchen," a wellness column in *The Wayfarer Magazine.* One of the inaugural Poets of Place for the lower St. Croix Valley, her poetry has been featured in numerous publications, including the St. Paul Almanac and South Dakota in Poems. She lives with her family in rural Minnesota, where they tend a large vegetable garden, explore nature, and do their best to live simply.

Apple Coffee Cake

- 3 large apples, peeled and cubed
- 1 ½ cups flour
- 2 ½ teaspoon baking powder
- ¾ teaspoon salt
- ½ cup sugar
- 1 egg, beaten
- ¼ cup butter, melted
- ½ cup milk
- ¼ cup applesauce
- For streusel topping:
- 2 teaspoons cinnamon, ¼ cup brown sugar, ½ cup flour, 3 tablespoons cold butter

Preheat the oven to 375. Sauté apples in a small saucepan with 1 tsp each of butter, sugar and cinnamon until softened. Set aside.

Combine butter, sugar and egg. Add milk and applesauce. Combine flour, baking powder and salt in another bowl and add to butter mixture, along with the apples. Pour into a greased 8x8 pan.

Combine cinnamon, brown sugar, flour and cold butter with a pastry blender and sprinkle over the top of the batter.

Bake for 45-55 minutes, or until a toothpick inserted into the middle comes out clean.

Be sure to pay attention to the scent of baking apples as you wait. Inhale the aroma of autumn. Exhale and move at whatever speed is necessary to step fully into the season.

www.ingramcontent.com/pod-product-compliance
Lightning Source LLC
Chambersburg PA
CBHW081005140626
46546CB00019B/3437